Table of Contents

Chapter 1: The Civilized Lie 1
Chapter 2: Echoes of the Arena 11
Chapter 3: The Child of the Tribe 19
Chapter 4: The Moral Performance Industry 27
Chapter 5: The Pathology of Progress 35
Chapter 6: The Return of the Sacred Enemy 45
Chapter 7: Exceptions or Excuses? 53
Chapter 8: Blood Is Conditional 61
Chapter 9: Loyalty Ends at Exposure 67
Chapter 10: The Death of the Inner Life 75
Chapter 11: Righteousness Is a Costume 85
Chapter 12: The Disappearing Self 95
Chapter 13: The War on Reality 107
Chapter 14: The Cult of the Good Person 119
Chapter 15: A Mirror Instead of a Flag 129

The Moral Illusion

The Rise of Performative Morality and
the Death of Honesty

Glenn Davies

Self Published

Copyright © 2025 Glenn Davies

The Moral Illusion The Rise of Performative Morality and the Death of Honesty
© 2025 Glenn Davies All rights reserved. No part of this publication may be reproduced, distributed, stored in a retrieval system, or transmitted in any form or by any means — electronic, mechanical, photocopying, recording, or otherwise — without the prior written permission of the author, except in the case of brief quotations used in critical articles, reviews, or educational settings. This is a work of nonfiction. All references to public events, systems, and ideologies are presented for commentary, critique, or analysis. Any resemblance to specific individuals is coincidental unless otherwise stated. First Edition: 2025 Self-Published. https://www.linkedin.com/in/daviesglenn/ For rights or licensing inquiries: glenn@cac-h2.com

Dedication

*For those who stopped clapping.
Who felt the lie tighten in their throat
and chose silence over safety.
Who stood alone in rooms full of
applause and whispered, "This isn't
real." For the ones who were exiled for
honesty,
called dangerous for asking questions,
or quietly erased for not nodding along.
For the ones who watched their own tribe
become everything it once condemned —
and walked away anyway. For those
who lost their place in the performance,
but found something more sacred in the
wreckage:
themselves.*

"Morality is the herd-instinct in the individual."

FRIEDRICH NIETZSCHE

Preface

You don't need to be evil to cause harm. You just need to need approval.

You don't need to lie. You just need to say what people expect. Smile when you're supposed to. Post what they post. Feel what the group feels — or at least pretend to. That's all it takes.

Because in today's world, morality isn't built. It's borrowed. It's performed. It's filtered through platforms, softened by slogans, measured by emotional response and social currency. We no longer speak to be honest. We speak to be safe.

We don't ask, *"What do I believe?"* We ask, *"What will they think?"* And so the self — the one that wrestles, doubts, contradicts, confesses — begins to rot in silence. Not because it was silenced by force, but because it was **rehearsed out of existence**.

This is not a book about evil. It's a book about something far more terrifying: **the slow death of conscience through constant performance**.

We are taught to be kind, to be good, to be righteous — but in practice, what we're trained to do is *act good enough to survive social judgment*. The result is a world filled with people who know how to signal virtue but not how to wrestle with it. We mimic the appearance of compassion while suppressing the discomfort of complexity. We praise the performance of grief while punishing honesty. We silence the individual in favour of the moral group costume.

And we do it all with a smile.

This book will talk about identity. About outrage. About silence, branding, reputation, cowardice, and applause. But none of it is really about *them*. It's about **you** — and what you become when your morality no longer comes from the inside, but from the eyes watching you.

If this book hurts, keep going. If you find yourself flinching, keep reading. The pain isn't punishment — it's proof that something inside you still remembers what the truth feels like.

And so the book begins, not with answers, but with a moment.
A real one.
One you will remember.
One you were told how to feel about before you ever asked what it meant.

Author's Note

This book is not meant to comfort.
It's meant to confront.

You won't find a guide for how to be a better person here — because the idea of being a "better person" has been industrialized into performance.

What you'll find instead is a mirror: clear, honest, and unfiltered.

If you find yourself resisting, aching, or uncomfortable while reading, good. That's where the truth usually begins.

— Glenn

Chapter 1

THE CIVILIZED LIE

"Civilization is a thin veneer, easily peeled away."

October 2023, Southern Israel.

The footage was grainy, filmed on a mobile phone. But what it showed was chillingly clear. Civilians — young people at a music festival — running, screaming. Gunfire in the background. Panic. Blood. Chaos.

A few hours later, a response would follow: airstrikes, buildings collapsing, lives crushed in seconds. The cycle had been reignited — but this time, the world was watching in high-definition, in real time.

Across Israel, people wept.

In Gaza, civilians celebrated.

Videos emerged of Palestinians & militants cheering the deaths of partygoers. Footage showed citizens chanting for vengeance, some demanding the total erasure of their enemies. Rationality evaporated. The discourse was no longer political — it was primal.

This wasn't about land. This was about religious identity, hatred, ideology, tribe, survival.

But here's the uncomfortable part: it wasn't confined to the region. Online, **millions of keyboard warriors across the globe** joined in — cheering death, mocking victims, demanding blood.

Humans with jobs, families, smartphones, and university degrees — howling for destruction, as if morality had a switch they could flip based on whose flag they supported.

These weren't fringe extremists. They were teachers, engineers, designers, students — people who, only days earlier, were posting about self-care, climate change, and corporate wellness.

Overnight, their feeds transformed into digital battlegrounds. Their profile pictures became flags. Their stories became propaganda. And their empathy became tribalized — parceled out based on allegiance, withheld based on ancestry. The ancient instinct had returned, cloaked in hashtags and high-speed internet.

What unfolded was not a war over truth, but a performance of moral alignment. To grieve too widely was betrayal. To pause was complicity. To humanize both sides was, somehow, a form of treason. People weren't just expressing opinions — they were auditioning for belonging, proving their worth to the online tribe.

And if you watched closely, you could see the shift: the eyes narrowed, the language hardened, and the boundary between "person" and "enemy" disintegrated.

This wasn't a regional conflict. It was a mirror — exposing how thin our moral evolution really is. The digital stage simply revealed what history has always shown: that beneath the costumes of modern civility, most people are still waiting for permission to dehumanize. Not because they are evil — but because they are afraid. And in fear, the tribe always comes first.

This is the lie.

This is the lie we tell ourselves: that we are civilized. That we are rational creatures, guided by evolved minds and restrained by moral wisdom. That empathy is our natural state — that it extends outward, without condition or bias, embracing all of humanity simply because we know better now.

But the truth is far darker. Empathy, for most people, is not universal — it's tribal. It is generous within the boundaries of the in-group but collapses quickly when the "other" enters the frame. We see this everywhere: in war zones where children are mourned on one side and dismissed as collateral on the other. In genocides, where once-friendly neighbors become targets. Even in comment sections, where people with full stomachs and steady lives still bay for blood under the veil of righteousness.

Because when humans feel threatened — when their identity, tribe, or worldview is cornered — the mask of moral progress slips. And what emerges isn't some enlightened 21st-century citizen, but a creature of the Bronze Age. The fire returns to the eyes. The fists clench. The urge to strike, to punish, to dominate, surges to the surface. All it takes is the right trigger — and the performance ends.

This is the central illusion of our time — that history is behind us, and we are something new. Because we wear suits instead of animal skins, hold smartphones instead of spears, and post slogans instead of chants, we've evolved beyond the tribal instincts that shaped our ancestors.

But moral behavior isn't inherited — it's performed. And when the stage collapses, the actor disappears, revealing something ancient underneath: a nervous system wired for survival, status, and submission to the tribe. The rest — the civility, the slogans, the smiling avatars — is costume. And in this book, I'm going to tear it off. Piece by piece. Layer by layer. Until we see what's been hiding underneath all along.

You don't need to travel to a battlefield to see it. You can find the tribal mind at work in boardrooms, in high schools, in political rallies, and in neighborhood WhatsApp groups. You can find it in how people choose sides in scandals they barely understand, or how they post black squares one month and forget the cause the next. You can see it in the way people suddenly speak with absolute certainty — not because they've studied an issue, but because their group has given them a script.

This is how modern tribalism operates: not through rocks and chants, but through algorithms, optics, and selective outrage. It rewards people for signaling the right beliefs, punishes those who hesitate or dissent, and builds a morality not on truth, but on cohesion. In such an environment, the goal isn't to understand — it's to belong. And nothing ensures belonging like a shared enemy.

That's why, in times of crisis, the speed with which people reduce entire populations to monsters isn't a flaw in modern thinking — it's a feature of ancient psychology. The tribe must have an enemy. And the enemy must be dehumanized, not just to justify violence, but to maintain the illusion that our side is still good.

The Neuroscience of Dehumanization

From a brain perspective, this isn't surprising. The *amygdala*, a small, almond-shaped cluster of nuclei located deep within the **medial temporal lobe** of the brain, is our primal fear center, which activates when we see someone as "the other." Studies show that **when people see images of out-group members suffering, their empathetic brain responses are significantly reduced** — or even absent. The circuitry of compassion is **not universal — it's selective**.

In Rwanda in 1994, people used machetes on their neighbors. In the Balkans, people turned on those they shared streets and schools with. In every case, the shift was not sudden — it was **always simmering under the surface**, needing only the right spark to explode.

We look back at history — Roman games, public executions, witch burnings — and we say, *"How could they?"* But the truth is: **they were us**. No different. Same DNA. Same fear responses. Same pack behavior. The only thing that's changed is the design of the tools.

Given the right conditions — fear, dehumanization, a permission structure — most of us are capable of monstrous acts.

This isn't cynicism. It's biology.

So What Is Civilization, Really?

It's not the accumulation of wisdom, nor the blossoming of moral maturity. It's not enlightenment in the philosophical sense — not a universal awakening of conscience. Civilization, at its core, is a framework. A system of rules, surveillance, and consequences that keeps our instincts in check.

It doesn't make us good — it makes us manageable. It builds walls around our darker tendencies, wraps them in etiquette, and calls the performance progress. But that performance is fragile. Civilization is not who we are — it's what we agree to pretend to be. It teaches us how to behave, but not always how to feel. When pressure breaks the system — through war, fear, humiliation, or loss — the costume drops.

Suddenly, beneath the language of politics or justice, we see the old reflexes: loyalty to tribe, hatred of the other, moral clarity replaced by ancestral instinct. The civilized mind is outrun by the ancestral brain. And it happens faster than most people are willing to admit.

You can witness this collapse every time rockets fly and children die. The world doesn't pause for facts. It doesn't wait for nuance. It splits. Immediately. Not based on evidence, but identity: Who is my tribe? Who is my enemy? Who should be grieved — and who can be written off as collateral? In the case of Israel and Palestine, that split is often instantaneous. The moral lens is not calibrated to justice — it's calibrated to allegiance. And once allegiance is fixed, all blood is filtered accordingly.

The Uncomfortable Origin: Religion, Not Politics

Ask most people what drives the Israeli–Palestinian conflict and they'll respond with the usual slogans: "It's about land." "It's colonialism." "It's apartheid."

But when you peel back the headlines and the hashtags, beneath the grief and the rubble lies something older than any political state, older than borders, and far more stubborn than ideology: religion.

Not just as a cultural force, but as **sacred text** — immutable, divine, and, in many cases, dangerously incompatible with coexistence.

The **Qur'an**, believed by Muslims to be the final and unalterable word of God, contains scores of references to Jews (approximately 60 versus with around 46 versus characterized by negative expressions of the Jews). Some acknowledge shared Abrahamic roots. Others reflect 7th-century political and tribal dynamics — betrayal, conflict, shifting alliances.

But many verses remain **unambiguously hostile**, cementing an image of Jews as cursed, treacherous, or spiritually diseased. These aren't fringe misinterpretations by a few extremists — they are read aloud in classrooms, chanted from pulpits, and recited as divine authority.

Among the verses most often cited by jihadist factions and militant clerics:

- "And humiliation and wretchedness were stamped upon them [the Jews], and they were returned with wrath from Allah…" — *Qur'an 2:61*
- "The worst of creatures in the sight of Allah are those who disbelieve…" — *Qur'an 8:55*
- "Whenever they kindled the fire of war [against you], Allah extinguished it…" — *Qur'an 5:64*

These verses, and dozens like them, are not symbolic or metaphorical within the theological mainstream. They are taught as truth. And here lies the core discomfort: **the text is immutable**. It cannot be revised. It is not interpreted in the elastic way modern liberal religions read their scriptures. To question the Qur'an's authority is to leave the faith. To deny its content is to blaspheme. This isn't extremism. It's orthodoxy.

And while many Muslims reject violence and coexist peacefully in pluralistic societies, surveys and sociological research have revealed a more troubling truth: **when pressed, loyalty to the *ummah* — the global Islamic community — overrides moral judgment.** In conflict, even secular Muslims almost exclusively side with the tribe. They may not pick up a weapon, but they will not condemn those who do. The silence is not neutral. It is allegiance.

This is why **Palestinian child indoctrination** is not a fringe issue — it is the operating system. In schools funded by *UNRWA* (the United Nations Relief and Works Agency), Palestinian children are taught martyrdom, resistance, and hatred of Jews as early as age five. Textbooks praise suicide bombers. Maps erase Israel entirely. Songs glorify blood and vengeance.

These are not isolated leaks — they are systemic features, well-documented by watchdog organizations and journalists brave enough to expose them. And they are **funded, in part, by Western tax dollars.**

The irony, of course, is staggering: Islam — an imperial religion that once colonized the land now called Israel — has positioned itself as the colonized. From the Umayyad conquests to the Ottoman occupation, Islamic power dominated the region for over a millennium. But now, in a post-colonial age where victimhood is currency, that history is erased. The conquering faith claims to be the oppressed. The aggressor becomes the martyr. And Western activists — mostly ignorant of theology or history — chant along, unaware that the cause they support includes verses that call for **their own destruction.**

This is not about anti-Muslim hatred. It is about moral honesty. If the conflict is to be understood — let alone resolved — we must stop pretending it's a disagreement over borders. It's a religious war, rooted in a theology that cannot be updated. A war not just of weapons and policies, but of holy words that command allegiance — even at the cost of peace.

Case Study: UNRWA Textbooks and the Manufacturing of Martyrs

In 2021, an investigation by the **Institute for Monitoring Peace and Cultural Tolerance in School Education (IMPACT-se)** revealed what many already suspected: that schools funded and operated by **UNRWA**, the United Nations agency tasked with educating Palestinian youth, were actively promoting violence, antisemitism, and martyrdom.

These weren't fringe educators. These were **state-sanctioned materials** used in classrooms across Gaza and the West Bank — printed with the UN logo, distributed to children as young as six. In one Grade 8 Arabic textbook, students were instructed to **identify Jews as the enemy** and glorify "heroic operations" (a euphemism for terror attacks). Maps of the region showed no trace of Israel. Exercises in grammar, math, and reading comprehension were infused with nationalist rhetoric, resistance themes, and violent imagery.

In a Grade 9 science book, Newton's laws were taught using slingshots aimed at IDF soldiers. In Islamic studies, martyrdom was framed not just as noble, but necessary.

Children were asked to **memorize and recite verses** that referred to Jews as monkeys and pigs — phrases lifted directly from Qur'anic interpretations. Heroic figures included **Dalal Mughrabi**, responsible for the Coastal Road Massacre that killed 38 Israeli civilians, including 13 children.

This isn't education. It's weaponization. And it's funded, in part, by Western governments — including the United States, Canada, the UK, the EU, and even Australia. When these revelations surfaced, there was international outcry — briefly.

But UNRWA offered denials, issued vague commitments to review content, and the funding continued. Why? Because confronting the truth would mean admitting that a system the West built to foster peace had become a **pipeline for holy war**.

Meanwhile, Hamas operates its own **summer camps** across Gaza. Children from ages 10 to 17 are trained in **military drills**, taught to handle firearms, chant antisemitic slogans, and memorize revolutionary songs. Some camps are overtly religious; others are cloaked in nationalist rhetoric. But the goal is the same: produce a generation that does not grieve for death — it aspires to it.

This is not an accident. It is a strategy. Hamas knows it cannot defeat Israel militarily — but it can raise children who will **die trying**, and it can shape international opinion by ensuring those deaths are televised. Children are taught not to dream, but to avenge. And in doing so, the cycle remains not just unbroken — but sacred.

The Global Mob Turns

What makes this conflict different is not just the complexity on the ground — but the brutal simplicity of global response.
In the weeks following October 2023, tens of thousands marched not just for peace, but for Israel's annihilation. Synagogues were attacked. Jewish students were harassed on campuses. In Western cities — in supposedly liberal democracies — the mob turned not on the killers, but the victims.

Educated, well-meaning professionals — graphic designers, teachers, medical students — posted memes **celebrating murder**. They cheered for the terrorists. They justified child killings. And when confronted, many **doubled down**, invoking decolonization, justice, or anti-Zionism — as if such terms could cleanse their bloodlust. Why?

Because the same instincts that drove **witch burnings** and **Roman arenas** are still with us. Only the names have changed. Only the hashtags have evolved.

Victimhood as Virtue, Power as Evil

We now live in a moral landscape where **power is guilt and victimhood is virtue**. In that paradigm, **Israel — for simply existing and defending itself — becomes "the oppressor"**, regardless of what actually happened. The psychology is tribal, not rational:

- *"I side with the one who appears weaker."*
- *"I believe the oppressed cannot be wrong."*
- *"I hate the one with tanks and jets."*

This is not justice. It is reflex masquerading as morality.
And when that moral identity is threatened, the reaction is not discourse — it is rage. Death threats. Boycotts. Mob fury.

This is not evolution. It is medievalism with a smartphone.

We Are Not Civilized. We Are Trained

There's a difference. Civilization teaches us the choreography of decency — when to speak, how to act, what to say in polite company. But beneath that training lies the same mind that howled in ancient valleys and sharpened stones for war. The conflict in Israel and Palestine doesn't just reveal geopolitical complexity — it exposes psychological simplicity. We are still wired for tribes. Still programmed to pick sides, chant slogans, and feel righteous as we demand blood.

We call it activism. We call it justice. But often, it is theatre. We don't engage issues — we perform identities. We don't examine — we affirm. Our posts are rituals, our outrage is currency, and our enemies are props in a moral pageant that masks something much older: the pleasure of vengeance. The hunger to punish. The relief of certainty in a world that feels increasingly out of control. This isn't new behavior. It is ancient. And disturbingly consistent across history, cultures, and creeds.

What's changed is not the impulse, but the interface. Our primal instincts have been rebranded in the language of progress. Hatred now wears hashtags. Retribution is wrapped in equity. And the thirst to destroy is baptized in the language of compassion. The packaging has evolved — the core has not. The same fire that once burned witches now burns reputations. The pyres are digital, but the scream is the same.

Foundational Texts, Foundational Divides

If we are to expose the raw core of the human condition, we must start at the source: **our holy books**. These texts are often held up as moral compasses. But dig beneath the poetry and metaphors, and you find something that echoes not peace — but **survivalism**, **tribal loyalty**, and the **violent exclusion of outsiders**.

The Qur'an: Immutable Hostility Toward the "Other"

The Qur'an is considered by Muslims to be the **direct, unchangeable word of Allah**, revealed through the Prophet Muhammad. It contains both spiritual guidance and explicit social-political instructions.

While the Qur'an offers verses of compassion and mercy, its **doctrine of duality** — kindness to believers, condemnation of disbelievers — is ever-present:

- *"Muhammad is the Messenger of Allah. And those with him are harsh against the disbelievers and merciful among themselves…"* (Qur'an 48:29)
- *"Fight those who do not believe in Allah…until they pay the Jizya with willing submission and feel themselves subdued."* (9:29)
- *"The Jews say: 'Uzair is the son of Allah'; and the Christians say: 'The Messiah is the son of Allah'… May Allah destroy them."* (9:30)

In Islamic jurisprudence, **abrogation** (naskh) allows later, more militant verses to supersede earlier peaceful ones. The result is a book that, when taken literally, **sanctions violence, institutionalizes inferiority of non-believers**, and fosters **eternal conflict with Jews and Christians** — the so-called *People of the Book*.

The Bible: From Genocide to Grace

The Christian Bible, particularly its Old Testament (shared with Judaism), is full of **tribal conquest, divine wrath, and moral absolutism**.

- *"Now go and strike Amalek and devote to destruction all that they have. Do not spare them, but kill both man and woman, child and infant…"* (1 Samuel 15:3)
- *"Happy is the one who seizes your infants and dashes them against the rocks."* (Psalm 137:9)

These are not fringe verses. They are foundational to a worldview where **God is tribal**, and moral action is defined by **obedience, not empathy**.

In the **New Testament**, the tone shifts — Jesus preaches love, humility, and forgiveness. Yet even here, duality persists:

- *"He who is not with me is against me…"* (Matthew 12:30)
- *"I did not come to bring peace, but a sword."* (Matthew 10:34)

Christianity evolved into a doctrine of spiritual salvation, but its institutions — crusades, inquisitions, colonization — **remained tools of domination**, often justified by scripture.

The Torah & Talmud: Law, Identity, and Outsiders

Judaism's foundational text — the Torah — is both legal code and origin story. It introduces **God as a protector of a chosen people**, who are given divine right to land, law, and superiority over pagan nations.

- *"When the LORD your God gives them over to you and you defeat them, you must devote them to complete destruction."* (Deuteronomy 7:2)
- *"You shall not intermarry with them…"* (Deut. 7:3–4)

The Talmud later expands on Jewish law and ethics, and is more interpretive. While often more humane in legal nuance, **early Judaism was a tribal religion concerned with survival and separateness**, not universal morality.

However, unlike Christianity and Islam, Judaism does **not evangelize**. Its violence is self-contained — **it excludes, but does not pursue**.

The Core Observation

Each of these books is **a mirror of its time** — a survival guide for desert tribes, not a universal charter of human rights. They reflect **fear, scarcity, identity, and power**. They offer:

- Kindness to insiders
- Obedience to God over ethics
- Hostility to outsiders
- Certainty over doubt

They are not moral because they are good — they are moral because **they say they are good**.

And they remain unchanged — immunized from reform by divine authority. This creates the most dangerous foundation for human conflict: a license to hate that cannot be revoked.

Modern Echoes, Ancient Voices

This is why the world splits so easily. Not because of data. Not because of justice. But because our **moral programming is tribal and scriptural**, not rational.

So when Gaza burns, and Tel Aviv bleeds, and New York marches, and London riots — what we are witnessing is not political disagreement. It is **religious inheritance colliding with modern identity politics**. The people cheering death on both sides are not monsters. They are **normal humans running ancient code**.

The Old Morality in New Clothing

We think we've moved on. That we've replaced sacred text with secular ethics. That we've evolved past violence into inclusion, compassion, and progressive values.

But we haven't.

We've just rebranded the same tribalism in the language of justice. Where once it was *"God wills it"*, **it is now** *"We are on the right side of history."*

Where once people called for death in the name of divine authority, now they call for destruction in the name of **anti-oppression, anti-colonialism, or anti-fascism** — without even understanding what those words mean.

Because it's not about meaning. It's about **alignment**. About **feeling righteous, superior,** and **safe in a moral tribe**.

This is why modern liberalism — particularly in the Western academy and cultural elite — has become **obsessed with victimhood**. Not because it cares for the weak, but because **victimhood is now power**. It confers authority, immunity, and status. In today's morality, **the more oppressed you are, the more righteous your anger becomes — and the more justified your hatred.**

Victimhood as Weapon: A Modern Case Study

After Hamas' unprecedented massacre in southern Israel, social media erupted. The violence was indiscriminate. Civilians were targeted. Children murdered. Entire families wiped out.

But within 48 hours, thousands of educated Westerners — lawyers, baristas, professors, students — began to post messages not of sympathy, but of celebration.

- "This is what decolonization looks like."
- "Israel had it coming."
- "By any means necessary."
- "Resistance is not terrorism."

None of these people would ever dream of beheading a civilian or shooting a baby. But they **cheered it**, in language borrowed from **social justice rhetoric**. They justified it with hashtags. They wrapped **ancient hatred in modern ideology**, and felt good about it.

This is the **civilized lie** at its most dangerous:

That **you are a good person** because you speak the right words — even as you excuse the most depraved actions.

They weren't radicalized jihadists. They were middle-class moralists, using iPhones and identity politics to repackage Bronze Age rage.

Case Study: The Stanford Prison Experiment (1971)

What happens when ordinary men are given roles of power or submission — and a tribe to protect?

> *In just six days, college students assigned to play "guards" in a simulated prison began abusing fellow students assigned as "prisoners." The cruelty escalated so rapidly that the experiment, meant to last two weeks, was shut down early. The takeaway: roles and context can override moral identity — quickly.*

◆ ◆ ◆

Chapter 2

ECHOES OF THE ARENA

*"We no longer gather in town squares.
We gather in threads."*

Rome: Blood and Bread

The Colosseum could hold 50,000 people. It was a marvel of architecture, engineering — and cruelty. For nearly 400 years, the Roman Empire fed its citizens a steady diet of violence as entertainment. Gladiator matches, executions, animal hunts — ritualized public death, not as deterrent, but as spectacle.

They didn't just kill criminals. They **orchestrated morality plays**:

- A slave who stole might be crucified dressed as a mythological traitor.
- A Christian might be dressed in lambskin and torn apart by lions in a mock Biblical parable.
- Prisoners reenacted war stories that ended in real beheadings.

These weren't isolated events. They were **social rituals**. Families attended. Vendors sold food. Senators applauded.

Why?

Because it satisfied something primal. It was the **externalization of punishment** — the **cleansing of guilt and fear through the destruction of another**. The same instinct that leads a pack of wolves to kill the sickest member to protect the whole.

Roman civilization wasn't failing when it built arenas. It was thriving — and **channeling its barbarism through structure and routine**.

Medieval Europe: Ropes, Fire, and the Mob

In medieval Europe, the arena changed. The **church replaced the emperor**, but the purpose remained: **control through public fear and participation.**

- **Witches were burned.** Not secretly, but in open fields, attended by crowds who believed they were witnessing righteousness in action.
- **Thieves were hanged** in town squares, sometimes left on display for days — their corpses reminders of order.
- **Heads were placed on spikes**, not just for warning, but for entertainment.

People brought their children. Vendors hawked meat pies. Songs were sung. **Public death was not horror — it was community theatre.** But perhaps most terrifying was that **everyone believed they were moral**. That watching someone suffer — if they were *bad enough* — made the town cleaner, safer, more whole.

Even when wrong. Even when innocent.

This wasn't justice. It was **ritualized cruelty wrapped in religious and legal justification** — the same core human mechanism the Romans had mastered, now baptized and robed.

Now we come to the present. We don't burn witches anymore.
We **cancel them. We dox them. We mock them. We ruin their lives.**
We tell ourselves we are enlightened. That we abhor violence. That we are better than the past.

But consider:

- A woman tweets a poorly phrased joke → within hours, she loses her job, receives rape threats, and becomes a global punchline.

- A celebrity missteps → within days, they are dragged through headlines, memes, think pieces, Reddit threads, YouTube exposés, and TikToks.
- Teenagers film fights in schools, humiliation, mental breakdowns — and upload them for **likes**, **views**, and **shares**.

No one dies. But many wish they had.

The pain is real. The punishment is public. And most disturbingly — **we enjoy it**.

We laugh. We share. We cheer.

Like Romans in the stands. Like villagers at the hanging tree.
But now we do it from our couches. With hashtags instead of stones.

Why We Love the Spectacle

Why are we so drawn to the downfall of others — to the drama, the shame, the public unravelling? Psychologists have a name for it: *moral outrage porn*. And it's not just a metaphor — it activates the same dopamine pathways in the brain as sugar, sex, or narcotics. It feels good. Righteous anger gives us a hit of superiority. It tells us we're better than *them*. That our flaws are minor. That we are on the right side of history. It doesn't just affirm our worldview — it relieves our private shame.

This is why outrage spreads so easily online. It offers a momentary escape from our own failings. The punished become avatars of our guilt. Their humiliation is a stand-in for our own self-hatred — only this time, we get to be the punisher. It's not justice we're seeking. It's purification.

We burn others in public hoping it will cleanse us in private. But what we're really engaging in is spiritual masturbation — a self-soothing ritual that simulates moral clarity without requiring actual introspection.

The ancient crowd used to gather in coliseums. Today, they gather in comment threads. The arena never closed — it just changed format. We no longer buy front-row seats with gold coins. We pay with our attention, our shares, our rage. The mechanics of the spectacle have evolved, but the emotion behind it remains disturbingly unchanged.

We don't clap for lions anymore. We retweet the attack. We don't chant for blood in person. We pile on anonymously. Yet beneath the screens and the polish and the virtue-signaling is the same primal delight: the thrill of righteous punishment, the hunger to watch someone fall, the deep, unspoken belief that some people deserve to suffer — and that we deserve to watch it happen.

This is not evolution. It's just rebranding. The fire still burns. Only the costumes have changed.

The Executioner Wears a Lanyard

It's tempting to believe that the people orchestrating public punishments today are fringe actors — extremists shouting from digital corners, or angry loners lost in ideological spirals. But that's not true. The modern executioner is far more ordinary. They are not hooded in shadows — they wear cardigans, carry laptops, and sip oat lattes in glass offices.

Today's moral punishers are embedded in polite society. They work in HR. In education. In tech firms and newsrooms. They attend DEI seminars and corporate mindfulness retreats. They know the correct pronouns, the trending causes, the words that must not be said, and the rituals that must be performed.

Their power isn't brute force — it's reputational annihilation. Their tools aren't gallows or guillotines, but Slack threads, email chains, and "community standards" policies.

They are the progressive journalists who campaign to blacklist an author for a decade-old tweet.
The teacher who calls out a student for misgendering in front of the entire class.
The academic with tenure who justifies looting as a form of "resistance."
The activist who posts someone's personal phone number online and calls it "accountability."

These people don't see themselves as cruel. On the contrary, they often believe they are righteous — warriors for justice, defenders of the oppressed, moral architects of a better world. And that is what makes them dangerous. **Because cruelty wrapped in virtue becomes unshakable.** The lash hurts more when the hand holding it is convinced it's doing good.

This is the most terrifying form of punishment: the kind carried out by people who sleep well after they ruin someone else's life. The kind that doesn't cause moral nausea — it triggers moral euphoria. The thrill of justice served. The pleasure of being seen as one of the good ones.

Ritual Punishment in "Safe" Spaces

Modern liberal societies have not abolished public punishment — they have **ritualized** it. The arenas have changed, but the architecture is the same. Where once there were coliseums and scaffolded platforms, we now have university campuses, HR departments, curated comment sections, and social media mobs. And in these spaces, the rituals of moral condemnation play out with eerie regularity.

First comes the initiation: a call to demonstrate allegiance — "Do the work." "Check your privilege." "Say the words." These aren't just social prompts; they are tests of submission. Say the wrong thing, or refuse to say anything at all, and the group grows suspicious.

Then comes the confession: "I now understand that I caused harm..." These statements are almost never organic. They are coerced, formulaic, and delivered not to the person harmed, but to the crowd. It is a ritual cleansing, scripted by pressure, not conscience.

Next is the punishment: cancellation, public apology, blacklisting, firing, deplatforming. The offender's social capital is removed. Their presence becomes radioactive. Companies erase their names. Publishers retract their books. Speakers are disinvited, accounts suspended, and reputations gutted.

And then the final stage: the crowd reaction. Not contemplation. Not grace. But **applause, memes, rage, hashtags, victory laps.** The crowd doesn't care about the offense — it cares about reaffirming its own virtue. The destruction isn't about restoring balance. It's about **elevating the mob.**

These rituals aren't justice. They're theatre. **Moral theatre.** Designed not to heal wounds, but to signal purity. Not to protect victims, but to confirm the tribe's moral supremacy. The crowd doesn't just want justice. It wants a show. And the offender's head — real or reputational — is the offering.

There's a phenomenon in social psychology known as **"moral licensing"** — the idea that after doing something "good," people often feel justified in doing something "bad."
In public punishment culture, we see something darker: **moral sadism.**

The psychological pleasure derived from watching someone be **publicly humiliated — when you believe they deserve it**.

This is **dopamine-fueled cruelty**. And it's addictive.

- It's why people who champion tolerance can be the most merciless to those who deviate from their script.

- It's why people who post "Be kind" will, hours later, demand someone's job over a 7-second video clip.
- It's why social justice spaces — meant to protect the vulnerable — often turn into digital firing squads.

We don't stone people anymore.
We "raise awareness."
We "hold them accountable."
We "protect the community."

But the result is the same: one person destroyed, a crowd applauding, and no one responsible.

What Makes It Worse Than Before

In ancient times, public executions were horrifying — but they were also **rare**, **geographically confined**, and **finite**. You had to be physically present to witness them. They happened in specific towns, on specific days, with specific victims. Once the spectacle ended, the crowd went home, and the condemned — however tragically — were allowed to disappear into history.

Today, public punishment is not only more common — it is **relentless**. One sentence, one image, one private message, or one out-of-context remark can become a permanent stain. A fleeting misstep becomes **an identity**, and that identity becomes **searchable**, **sharable**, and **endlessly monetizable** by media algorithms. There are no gallows now — just archives. And no expiration date. What was once executed is now indexed.

The executioner has evolved too. They no longer wear hoods or wield axes. They are anonymous, invisible, and infinite. A single mistake can summon a **million digital punishers**, none of whom know the accused, none of whom are accountable, and all of whom believe they are doing good. It's not just the cruelty that's horrifying — it's the **certainty**. Every swipe, every share, every retweet is carried out with absolute moral confidence. There are no doubts. Only sides.

And worse still — **participation is now currency**. The internet has taught us not only to accept these rituals, but to enjoy them. **To be seen as punishing is to be seen as virtuous.** That's why people don't just watch — they join. They comment, pile on, repost, amplify. They don't even need to believe what they're saying. They just need the signal — the chance to belong to the righteous crowd.

We've **outsourced cruelty** to the hive mind, and taught millions to wear that cruelty like a badge. The more creative the destruction, the more viral the righteousness. And because there's no blood, no corpse, no physical cost — only digital ruin — people feel absolved. No one thinks they're the executioner. They think they're the moral accountant. The reckoning. Justice. And they sleep soundly.

But the damage is worse than before. **There is no death — only digital exile.** The condemned are not buried. They're frozen in place, day after day, on Google search results, on screenshots, in memes and comment threads. Their careers collapse. Their social circles dissolve. Their name becomes a cautionary tale. A ghost story told to keep others obedient. And the mob? It moves on. It always does. Hungry for its next sacrificial high.

◆◆◆

Case Study: Bret Weinstein and the Day Dissent Became Heresy

In 2017, **Bret Weinstein**, a biology professor at **Evergreen State College**, became the center of a media firestorm — not for anything he did violently or abusively, but for a **polite email**.

Each year, Evergreen held a symbolic event called the **"Day of Absence,"** where Black students and faculty voluntarily absented themselves from campus to highlight their contributions and experiences. It was a protest of presence by absence — and Weinstein supported it.

But that year, the event changed: instead of Black students leaving campus voluntarily, **white students and faculty were "encouraged" to stay off campus**. It reversed the symbolism — from voluntary solidarity to coerced segregation. Weinstein wrote a respectful email voicing concern:

> "There is a huge difference between a group voluntarily absenting themselves from a shared space in order to highlight their vital roles... and a group encouraging another group to go away."

That was it. No slurs. No aggression. Just dissent — the kind of civil, thoughtful disagreement a university is supposed to welcome.

But what followed was chaos.

Protests erupted. Students mobbed his classroom. They screamed at him, branded him a racist, and demanded his resignation. Campus security told him they could no longer guarantee his safety. He had to hold office hours in a public park. The college president did nothing to de-escalate the crisis. And eventually, Weinstein and his wife — also a professor — **were forced to resign**.

Not because he was hateful. Not because he broke a rule. But because he questioned the new moral orthodoxy. And that was enough. His refusal to participate in the ritual was interpreted as an attack on the tribe. And so the tribe did what tribes do: it expelled the heretic.

Bret Weinstein lost his job, his community, and his reputation in academic circles. And yet, even years later, many still label him a bigot —

despite a record of lifelong progressive activism. Why? Because nuance no longer matters in a performance culture. **The punishment was the point.**

There Is No End to This Hunger

The problem with mobs isn't that they punish injustice — it's that they don't stop once the punishment is delivered. They keep going. The moment the target is destroyed, the hunger returns. Louder. Emptier. Desperate for something — someone — to devour.

The dopamine hit of outrage is fleeting. And so, to feel it again, the moral lines must shift.

- Yesterday's ally becomes today's heretic.
- Yesterday's joke becomes today's hate speech.
- Yesterday's silence becomes today's crime.

And no one is safe — not even the architects of the scaffold. You can help build the arena, enforce the rules, chant all the right slogans, and still be dragged into the center when the rules change — because **they always do**. When a society begins to equate righteousness with retribution, every citizen is a future sacrifice.

We like to believe that cruelty is an infection — something introduced from the outside, something unnatural. We blame institutions, ideologies, and failed parenting. We tell ourselves that hatred must be taught, that moral sadism is learned. But this is a comforting myth.

Cruelty does not need to be taught. It needs only opportunity.

Watch children on a playground long enough and you'll see it: the forming of cliques, the exclusion of the weak, the delight in someone else's shame. No manifesto. No training. Just instinct. The lines are drawn before they even know what a country is. Long before they understand politics or religion or race, they've already learned to wound, to deceive, to divide.

Because they didn't need to be taught.

They were simply waiting for permission.

Chapter 3

THE CHILD OF THE TRIBE

"You weren't taught to exclude. You were born to."

Tribalism Is Not Taught — It's Felt

We tell ourselves that children are blank slates. That they arrive innocent, unformed, waiting to be shaped by culture, education, and experience. We imagine them as morally neutral — little bundles of potential who must be taught to hate, taught to exclude, taught to divide.

But walk onto a schoolyard before the age of ten, and you'll see the truth.

Children form tribes instinctively. No one tells them to. No one has to. They cluster to sameness like iron filings to a magnet. They group by accent, clothing, strength, race, posture — anything that signals who is "us" and who is "them." Those who don't fit are not reasoned with. They are mocked. Ignored. Isolated. Dominance isn't argued — it's performed. Power is worshipped, weakness is punished, and difference is feared before it's understood.

They don't know what politics is. But they understand rank.
They don't grasp ideology. But they grasp belonging.
And long before they know what cruelty means, they know exactly how to wield it.

Science has caught up. **Evolutionary psychology** has shown that by the age of five:

- Children **prefer** those who speak with familiar accents.
- They **trust** faces and voices that resemble their own.
- They **favor** those who conform to superficial group norms — even shirt color or snack choice.
- And most disturbingly: they **smile** when someone who breaks those group rules is punished.

This is not socialization. This is software. **Hard-coded. Default. Pre-installed.**

We don't need to teach children to fear the outsider. We need to teach them not to. And even then, it barely works. Because the pull of the tribe is not just cultural — it is **neurological**. It is a survival instinct dressed in social language. It is the ghost of the savannah whispering that loyalty equals life, and difference equals threat.

And if you watch closely, you'll see that childhood cruelty doesn't arise from evil. It arises from **pattern recognition**. Children mimic power. They follow hierarchy. They sense who can be hurt without consequence. And they hurt them.

What begins in the sandbox becomes policy in adulthood. What starts as teasing becomes online pile-ons, party politics, cultural warfare. The only thing that changes is the vocabulary.

And perhaps the most terrifying truth of all is this:
The child who bullies isn't broken.
The child who excludes isn't corrupted.
They are simply **tapping into the oldest operating system the human mind has ever known** — one that predates civilization, morality, and religion.

The tribe.

Case Study: The Puppet Test

In one famous Yale study, children watched two puppets play a game. One puppet cheated. The children were then asked:
"What should we do to the puppet who cheated?"
Many said: "Punish him."
Some said: "Take away his toy."
A disturbing number said: "Cut off his head."

They weren't angry.

They were smiling.

The urge to destroy **the rule-breaker** — to cleanse the tribe of the deviant — was not something they reasoned their way into.

It was **something they felt. Naturally.**

Bullying and the Morality of Groups

A child who punches another without reason is not the most dangerous figure on the playground. He's obvious — impulsive, visible, easy to discipline. The real danger is subtler. It's the group standing nearby — silent, giggling, watching.

Not because they're evil. But because they're learning.

They're absorbing the most enduring moral lesson of human civilization: **If the group permits it, it must be right.** If no one intervenes, the cruelty must be deserved. If the victim is silent or weak, then the pain must be their fault. These children aren't becoming monsters — they're becoming *members*. Members of a tribe that rewards loyalty, punishes dissent, and measures right and wrong not by conscience, but by consensus.

In that moment, the child's mind rewrites the event in language that will follow them into adulthood:

- "She asked for it."
- "They had it coming."
- "It's not bullying — it's just consequences."

Each laugh, each shrug, each refusal to act is not passive. It is **instructional**. It teaches hierarchy. It teaches immunity. It teaches the terrifying idea that **justice is determined by social approval**, not principle.

And if no adult interrupts that lesson — if no one names what happened, protects the victim, or rebukes the tribe — then the logic hardens. It becomes law. The cruelty no longer feels like an exception. It feels like order.

That is how moral passivity breeds cultural rot.
Not through the malice of the few — but through the silence of the many.
And those who laughed at the bullied child become the adults who laugh at the fallen politician, the cancelled stranger, the disgraced colleague — never questioning why, only relieved that it wasn't them.

Because the lesson was never about kindness.
It was about survival.
And the tribe never forgets who clapped — and who spoke out.

How Parents Train Children to Pretend

Parents rarely teach empathy. Not truly. What they teach — often with the best intentions — is *the appearance* of empathy. They teach tone, posture, and timing. They coach social choreography: how to behave like someone who cares, whether you do or not.

"Say sorry."
"Use your nice voice."
"Share, even if you don't want to."

These aren't lessons in compassion. They're **scripts**. And the child, eager to avoid scolding or earn approval, begins to memorize them. Quickly, they learn that sincerity is optional — what matters is *performance*. That kindness is not a feeling, but a gesture. That saying the right thing at the right moment is more important than meaning it.

So the child adapts. Not morally, but socially. They become actors. Smiling when told. Apologizing on cue. Performing warmth. And in return, they are rewarded: praise, affection, relief. The lesson is clear — **virtue is appearance**. Goodness is not something you are. It's something you wear.

This is how adult hypocrisy is born. In living rooms, classrooms, and playgrounds. Not in malice — but in mimicry. We grow up believing that the goal is not to *be* good, but to be **seen** as good. To say the right words, adopt the correct posture, nod at the proper outrage. Even when the heart feels nothing.

And so we become fluent in **moral fluency** — not moral feeling. We become experts in empathy theater. And we teach the next generation to do the same.

Not because we are evil. But because we were taught to smile before we could understand why.

By middle childhood, kids become masters of **reputation management**. They tattle selectively. They lie convincingly. They **mirror adult language** to justify cruelty:

- *"He was being annoying."*
- *"She said something racist."*
- *"He's not like us."*

They weaponize identity, manipulate emotion, and **test moral boundaries — not to learn what's right, but to see what they can get away with.** The child does not evolve into the mob. The mob is the child, with a bigger vocabulary. And so the loop closes.

The adult in the Twitter thread, demanding someone be fired, is the same child who laughed when a classmate was pushed down. The HR executive who performs moral outrage is the same kid who tattled selectively to win points.

The protester who cheers for violence is the same playground tyrant — just better dressed, better armed with language, but no less tribal, no less cruel. We did not outgrow the arena. We just grew tall enough to build our own.

The Adolescent Brain Needs a Tribe

The adolescent brain is a machine built for allegiance.

Biologically, it's half-formed — the **prefrontal cortex**, responsible for rational thought, emotional regulation, and impulse control, is one of the last regions to mature, often not fully functional until the mid-twenties. That's the part of the brain that allows an adult to pause and say: *"Maybe I'm wrong."* But adolescents don't pause. They charge.

Because before the rational mind is fully online, the emotional engine is running hot — driven by two overpowering forces:

- **The need for peer approval**
- **The desperate search for identity**

It's the perfect storm. A mind already wired for tribalism, now biologically desperate to **belong**, but unable to self-regulate, slow down, or examine its own ideas. And in a world where the old tribes — geography, family, religion, culture — have fractured or faded, young people go searching for **new flags to wave**. They don't want ideas. They want **belonging with a mission**.

And so they find it — not in person, but online. Not in community, but in ideology.

In the digital era, identity is a click away. And ideology becomes the new village. Political movements, social justice crusades, gender activism, religious radicalism, even video game fandoms — all offer the tribal scaffolding a young person craves.

Each one speaks a language:

- *"Problematic."*
- *"Gaslighting."*
- *"Based."*

- *"Silence is violence."*

Each one offers rituals: hashtags, black squares in the BLM movement, pile-ons, cancellation campaigns. Each has its sacred texts — viral videos, manifesto posts, weaponized threads. And each has **heretics** — those who question the dogma, hesitate to speak, or voice nuance. They are not debated. They are destroyed.

Why? Because ideology doesn't offer answers — it offers **identity**. And to a teenager who has no stable self, no history, no grounding, the ability to say "I am with this" is intoxicating. It provides more than clarity. It provides **certainty**. And more importantly: **moral immunity**.

Because if your tribe is good, then *you* are good.
No introspection required. No growth demanded. Just **alignment**. You do not need to be ethical — only consistent. You do not need to be kind — only correct.

This is not moral evolution. It is **shortcut sanctity**.

A century ago, a sixteen-year-old with radical views might have scribbled in a diary, argued with friends, or shouted into the void. Today, that same adolescent can broadcast their certainty to **millions**. In seconds. With amplification, affirmation, and zero accountability.

Social media **rewards** the worst traits of the undeveloped mind. It thrives on outrage, purity, speed, and tribal loyalty — all traits adolescents possess in abundance. And it **punishes** the traits they haven't yet learned: doubt, patience, moderation, humility.

So we get high schoolers issuing moral proclamations on race, war, and economics — not because they understand, but because they're fluent in the slogans. We get college students demanding speakers be banned, books be burned, history be rewritten — not because they're authoritarian, but because they're **terrified of being excluded**. We get young adults joining digital mobs — not out of hatred, but out of **a fear far deeper than cruelty**: the fear of being alone.

They aren't monsters.

They're adolescents with a megaphone, incentivized to moral extremism by the algorithms that feed them.
And they're terrified — not of being wrong, but of being **cast out**. What we are witnessing is not moral growth. It is **emotional regression with global reach**.

And every time we applaud it — every time we platform it, reward it, echo it — we turn the most vulnerable minds into moral soldiers for causes they don't even understand.

Because at that age, they don't want truth. They want a tribe that will keep them safe — as long as they stay loyal.

A Real Case: The Virtue Siege on Campus

In 2021, at a well-known Australian university, a philosophy lecturer introduced a unit on ethical pluralism. During the lecture, he presented various real-world moral dilemmas — including controversial legal cases — and asked students to explore **conflicting perspectives** without judgment. He quoted Aboriginal philosophers. He referenced Enlightenment thinkers. He stressed the value of **debating uncomfortable ideas**.

By evening, student unions had:
- **Accused him of "creating an unsafe space"**
- Published an open letter claiming he had **"platformed colonial logic"**
- **Demanded the university retract his materials and issue a formal apology**

No one had engaged the arguments. No one had challenged him intellectually.
Instead, they **performed collective injury** — because on that campus, **expressing moral discomfort was the currency of belonging**.

It wasn't education.
It was a **ceremony of ideological immunity**, where emotional safety replaced intellectual courage.

Friendship as Ideology, Not Intimacy

Even friendship — once the last refuge of authenticity in youth — has become politicized. Where children once bonded over laughter, games, or proximity, young people today are taught, directly or by osmosis, to choose friends based on **ideological alignment**.

- Do you believe in the right cause?
- Have you posted the right message of support?
- Did you ever say the wrong word, even once?

One misstep — one pause, one outdated opinion — and the friendship becomes a **threat**, not just to one's social circle, but to tribal survival. The fear isn't rooted in emotional betrayal. It's reputational. Because in this new morality of optics, friendship is no longer about closeness — it's about cover. It's not about who knows your heart. It's about who protects your standing.

So teenagers and young adults adapt. They filter. They perform.
They say what they must, not what they mean.
They echo outrage they don't feel, and recite slogans they don't believe.

Not because they're dishonest, but because they're afraid. **Afraid of exile.**
Afraid of becoming the next target.

And the most tragic part? In mimicking the tribe to stay safe, they become the very mob they fear. The cruelty is no longer external. It's internalized.

From the playground to the protest.
From the sandbox to the subreddit.
From the lunchroom to the campus quad.

The instincts remain unchanged:
- **Loyalty over truth**
- **Belonging over integrity**
- **Punishment over understanding**

Adulthood doesn't strip the tribe from the child. It simply **elevates** it — gives it a banner, a vocabulary, a justification. It teaches the child how to clothe ancient instincts in modern language. They don't become less tribal. They become more **strategically tribal**.

And if you still believe that morality is something we choose freely — that children learn to hate only through corrupt parents or failed institutions — look to the clearest historical proof that identity can be formed long before conscience ever has a chance to grow.

Case Study: Hitler Youth (1930s–40s)

The Hitler Youth was not just an indoctrination program. It was **moral engineering**. A system designed to ensure that children aligned with ideology before they could form their own beliefs. Boys and girls were conditioned to place **the tribe above truth**, obedience above thought, and party loyalty above family bonds.

They were taught to report their parents.
To chant slogans they didn't understand.
To see their ethnicity not as heritage — but as **sacred identity**.

By adolescence, many were turning in neighbors and teachers for ideological disloyalty — not because they were naturally cruel, but because they believed they were **doing the right thing**. Not because they were coerced — but because they were convinced.

They didn't feel brainwashed.
They felt **righteous**.
They weren't ashamed.
They were **proud**.

That's the danger. When tribal loyalty is cemented before moral reasoning has matured, a child will **destroy with joy** — believing they are a hero.

The tribe didn't disappear. It just evolved.
Its slogans are new. Its tools are digital.
But its pull on the human mind is just as old — and just as powerful.

The child never left the playground.
They just **brought the playground to the world**.

Chapter 4

THE MORAL PERFORMANCE INDUSTRY

*"We haven't built a better world.
We've built a better stage."*

Virtue Is the New Currency

In today's attention economy, outrage is capital, and capital demands growth. Every click, comment, hashtag, and boycott isn't just emotional release — it's a financial transaction. Morality has been monetized. And in this new market, virtue is no longer lived — it's leveraged.

Corporations no longer sell only products. They sell alignment. They sell values. They sell the illusion of collective conscience — neatly packaged in a campaign, an ad, a tweet.

A bank doesn't need to offer you security — it just needs to show you a rainbow logo during Pride Month. A tech company doesn't need to protect your privacy — it just needs to post about "equity" on Instagram. A clothing brand doesn't need to raise wages — it just needs to feature one "empowered" model and a tagline about body positivity.

This isn't moral leadership. It's moral theatre — and we're all paying for front-row seats.

The shift is subtle but corrosive. Ethics used to be about actions. Now, it's about aesthetics. The right phrases. The right timing. The right posture of contrition. Not because anyone changed — but because someone was watching.

In this new performance economy, corporations don't take risks to do what's right — they calculate what appears right to the largest number of people for the lowest possible cost. They don't lead moral revolutions — they follow moral trends, adopting slogans like seasonal fashion, abandoning them just as easily when the next marketable crisis arises.

And the public, desperate to feel good without doing good, rewards the performance. A single photo of an executive kneeling. A two-minute ad featuring a multiracial cast and soft piano music. A tweet condemning the thing everyone is already condemning. These are not acts of courage.

They are safety plays — ritual displays of moral conformity disguised as progress.

The companies know exactly what they're doing. They know that identity is now the most powerful brand loyalty program on Earth. And so they manufacture the feeling of shared values — not because they hold them, but because they know you will.

They hire consultants, launch DEI task forces, issue word-filtered statements vetted by lawyers. Behind closed doors, nothing changes. But in public, they shine. Because modern consumers no longer just buy products — they buy the illusion of righteousness.

It's not about who you are. It's about how your moral performance makes them feel about themselves.

What's most sinister is that this industry doesn't just exploit morality — it erodes it. When everything becomes a brand, nothing is sacred. Empathy becomes a marketing strategy. Apologies become PR plays. Diversity becomes an advertising metric.

We're no longer moved by conscience — we're moved by metrics.

And worst of all, the truly ethical — those who speak without scripts, act without cameras, resist the crowd's whims — are often left unseen, unsupported, and dismissed. Because genuine virtue is quiet. It's inconvenient. It doesn't trend.

But performance? That scales.

This is not about change. It's about appearing changed. Not about ethics. About optics.

In this economy, you don't have to be moral. You just have to look a little more moral than your competitors.

Corporate Woke-Washing

They call it **woke-washing** — the practice of borrowing the language of justice to protect capital. To wear morality like makeup. To package ethics in ad copy and campaign slogans while the machinery underneath remains untouched.

You've seen it.

A fast fashion brand launches a women's empowerment line — while paying female workers in Bangladesh less than a dollar an hour.
An oil company floods your feed with green slogans — while financing offshore drilling and lobbying against carbon accountability.
A multinational bank pins Black Lives Matter hashtags to its Twitter profile — while quietly redlining minority communities and denying generational wealth access for decades.

These aren't contradictions. They're **strategy**.

Woke-washing is not a glitch in the system. It *is* the system. A system that has learned how to hijack the language of progress — not to change, but to **survive**. When morality becomes a brand asset, **sincerity becomes obsolete**. The public no longer asks, *"Are they ethical?"* They ask, *"Did they say what I needed to hear, in the tone that makes me feel affirmed?"*

And the corporations deliver. Not with courage — but with consultants. With legal teams, brand analysts, and optics strategists. Not to **mean** something. But to **appear** as though they do.

In this ecosystem, the goal isn't to tell the truth.
The goal is to manage perception.
Not to *be* aligned — but to *signal* alignment.
Not to correct injustice — but to inoculate against criticism.
It is not leadership. It is **preemptive appeasement**.

Because the crowd no longer wants integrity. It wants performance. And the fastest way to secure brand safety is not with action, but with allegiance.

And then there's the media — once entrusted with truth, now addicted to **outrage as currency**.

The media doesn't report the world. It **curates emotion**.

Every headline is an engineered product, not designed to inform, but to trigger engagement. And what engages most? Not balance. Not nuance. Not complex analysis. But tribalism. Fury. Indignation. Articles are crafted to spark:
- Clicks
- Shares
- Rage
- Loops of moral offense that reinforce identity

You don't read the news anymore. You *join* it — as a participant in a performance. A performance where the story doesn't matter unless there's a villain. A performance where you're invited not to think — but to **cheer the destruction of someone else**.

And journalists? They've adapted. Many have gone from seekers of truth to **performers of purity**, crafting content not to expose reality, but to please a crowd that demands alignment. They fear the mob like everyone else — and so they speak in code. They write in hashtags. They flatten nuance into headlines that fit the tribe's needs. They stop asking hard questions. Because hard questions don't trend. But moral certainty does.

And so the sacred institutions that once held power accountable now **serve** it — disguising appeasement as activism, and conformity as courage.

This is not journalism. This is **content warfare** — a culture not of inquiry, but of ritualized outrage.

When corporations and media alike abandon sincerity for performance, what hope is there for truth? When morality is **marketed**, who dares to actually live it?

Because in a world of moral theatre, the loudest actor wins — and the crowd doesn't care if the script is fake.

Universities: Morality as Compliance

Once upon a time, the university was a sanctuary for dangerous ideas. A forge for critical thinking. A place where you could test your mind against better ones — and either sharpen it or watch it fail. But the modern university has abandoned that mission. It no longer teaches students how to think. It teaches them how to comply.

Professors spew propaganda. Students police language like border guards. Administrators issue apologies before the offense even happens. Inquiry has been replaced with ritual. Disagreement is framed as harm. Silence is treated as guilt. Every conversation is subject to interpretation — and every interpretation has a moral score.

Classrooms that once held debate now host confession.
The goal is not truth — it is emotional safety.
Courses are not built around questions — they are built around **identity quotas**.

Ideas are no longer tested by fire. They are ranked by **acceptability**, approved only if they align with the prevailing dogma. The result? A generation of graduates trained not in wisdom, not in discernment, but in

moral mimicry. Not free thinkers — but highly educated **performers**. And diplomas? They're no longer a testament to knowledge. They're a certificate of **conformity** — proof that the student learned the lines, played the part, and never made the tribe uncomfortable.

But this rot is not confined to the ivory towers.

Even the nonprofit world — the arena where real virtue should thrive — has succumbed to performance. Charities now **brand suffering** for Western donors. Campaigns reduce impossibly complex crises into two-minute videos and guilt-drenched taglines. Victims are flattened into helpless icons. Aid becomes a theatre of Western salvation, complete with dramatic music and staged photos of gratitude.

Impact becomes hard to verify. Staff burnout becomes routine. Turnover is constant. And beneath it all lies an uncomfortable truth: many nonprofits have stopped doing real service — and started doing **empathy laundering**.

They offer not help, but **relief** — not to the suffering, but to the donor.

They sell the feeling of goodness to those who need to believe they're good. They offer moral absolution in exchange for a subscription fee, or a click, or a bracelet. It is not justice. It is a brand.

And like any brand, it must evolve. The campaigns must be updated. The slogans must stay current. The causes must rotate to match public appetite. Because this isn't about solving the crisis. It's about staying *relevant* within it.

This is not service.
It is **performance**.
And performance — like fashion — must always be seasonal.

The moral performance industry works because it **exploits ancient psychological drives**:

- The desire to belong
- The fear of exclusion
- The craving for status
- The hunger for an enemy

But it does so with modern technology and global reach.
A university used to shape the minds of hundreds.
Now, a tweet from its DEI office shapes the mood of millions.
A commercial used to sell soap.
Now, it sells salvation.
The impulse is ancient.
The platform is global.
And the **ritual of moral display** has never been more profitable.

The Dangers of a Performance-Based Morality

When morality becomes a performance instead of a principle, something quietly catastrophic happens.

It disconnects from consequence.
It becomes **immune to evidence**, and **hostile to truth**.
It is no longer measured by real-world outcomes, but by optics, slogans, and emotional resonance.

In this theater of virtue, **cruelty is no longer recognized as cruelty** — because it wears the costume of moral justice.

- Censorship is justified as protection.
- Vengeance is rebranded as accountability.
- Silencing is reframed as safety.

And no one is allowed to ask: *"Is this good?"*
Only: *"Is this aligned?"*

Because in a morality built for display, **purity becomes the product**, and the tribe becomes the judge. And the moment ethics become a commodity, **conscience dies in the name of conformity**.

Language — once the vehicle for truth — becomes the primary instrument of control.

We no longer use words to illuminate. We use them to **signal**. To gatekeep. To obscure. To divide.

Modern institutions no longer teach people to **act rightly**. They teach people to **speak correctly**. Goodness is not a function of what you do — it's a function of whether you say the thing, in the tone, with the right inflection, and the right hashtags.

The result is a surreal moral landscape:
- People are fired for using the wrong phrasing, even when their intent was harmless.
- Others are celebrated for completely hollow declarations — as long as they deliver them in the **morally approved dialect**.

Words like *"harm," "safety," "ally," "equity," "justice,"* and *"diversity"* have become **totemic**. Their meanings are no longer stable — they are **inflated with tribal power** and **emptied of precision**. They are no longer tools for communication. They are **passcodes** into moral belonging.

To say them is to signal safety.
To ask what they mean is to invite suspicion.
To critique them is to court exile.

This is not language as discourse. This is **language as tribal currency** — a code, a shield, and a sword all at once.

And once moral belonging is determined not by your *actions*, but by your *phrasing*, we've entered a world where ethics are reduced to **linguistic choreography** — a dance of performative empathy, where sincerity is optional, but **fluency in the code is mandatory.**

The result is a culture fluent in moral language but starved of moral courage.

Performative Activism: Virtue as Brand

In an age where image outweighs intention, and visibility supersedes virtue, morality has become currency — a thing to be traded, curated, and broadcast. What once came from the soul is now crafted by the algorithm. Being good is no longer about doing good; it's about appearing aligned. Optics are everything. Alignment is everything. Performance is everything.

You see it every day. A tech CEO speaks solemnly of inclusion while quietly eliminating entire teams. A fashion brand champions women's empowerment in its advertising — while exploiting female garment workers in unregulated factories. A celebrity livestreams tears over injustice — framed carefully within the marble backdrop of a luxury home. A multinational corporation pins a trending cause to its social feed, while lobbying behind closed doors to protect exploitative supply chains.

This isn't activism. It's choreography. And it works.

Because in this new reality, the public has been trained to reward display over depth. We don't ask, "Do they act with integrity?" We ask, "Did they say the thing I like, in the way I needed to hear it?" Morality is no longer measured by consequence — only by emotional satisfaction.

And it's not just corporations. Individuals have learned the same game. The good person is now a personal brand — a social performance designed for protection and leverage. Righteousness becomes a career asset. Wokeness becomes a shield. Posting, speaking, signaling — all curated for reward. Followers. Jobs. Panels. Praise. Safety.

Intent is no longer relevant. Action is negotiable. All that matters is projection.

This is why we now live in a culture where cruelty can be celebrated, if the wording is correct — and kindness can be condemned, if phrased the wrong way. Apologies are demanded not for harm, but for deviation. Success belongs to those who master the dialect of performance — who know how to recite the lines, avoid the landmines, and deliver outrage or empathy with algorithmic precision.

No one wants truth. Truth doesn't trend. They want moral confirmation — and they want it packaged in the format of social entertainment.

The Mirror That Watches Back

In this world, there are no private thoughts — only deferred liabilities. Every message can be screenshotted. Every statement can be reframed. Every silence can be politicized. There is no forgiveness — only memory. And there is no privacy — only the illusion of it.

We've constructed a society where people speak in code, not conviction. Where colleagues monitor one another like informants. Where moral alignment is gauged not by contribution, but by posture. Where everyone lives in a state of low-grade performance anxiety — constantly asking themselves not "Am I right?" but "Am I next?"

This isn't Orwell's boot stamping on a face. It's a thousand polite faces watching you carefully, silently judging, endlessly recording — waiting to see if you'll slip. Waiting to see if your performance falters. Waiting to see if you're pure enough today.

And when someone does fall — when someone tweets the wrong thing, or says the unsanctioned truth — the crowd doesn't pause. It celebrates. A ritual feeding frenzy begins. Not because they were hurt. But because they were hungry.

In 2021, a woman named Emily, a mid-level editor at a publishing house, tweeted a single line after a long and frustrating day: "Sometimes I think we care more about identity checklists than good writing. No one wants to say it out loud." She said it out loud.

Within six hours, the punishment machine roared to life. Her tweet was flagged, circulated, condemned. A petition was created. Anecdotes emerged. Former interns stepped forward with vague accusations. Her company apologized. She was suspended. Then "quietly" removed.

But the machine didn't stop with her. It never does. It continued with those who condemned her. They gained followers. They appeared on podcasts. They gave interviews about justice and inclusion — positioning themselves as thought leaders in the morality marketplace.

Emily vanished. The performers rose.

Her fall wasn't about accountability. It was about fuel. The machine runs on sacrifice — and the spectacle of sacrifice is what feeds the crowd.

This is no longer a society. It's a morality content economy.

Outrage is a business model. Empathy is an aesthetic. Justice is a trending filter. And those who understand the algorithm best — those who know how to surf the emotional currents of the crowd — become its new priests.

And the real victims? They're irrelevant. The real oppressors? Untouchable. What matters is that someone bleeds and someone posts about it. Because the show must go on.

It's not enough to act morally. You must *appear* moral. And if you can't — you will be replaced by someone who can.

But this phenomenon doesn't stop with individuals. It metastasizes outward — into NGOs, universities, governments, and global diplomacy. Institutions that once existed to serve now exist to *signal*. The language of service has been replaced by the optics of moral ritual.

Charities sell suffering as branding. Universities teach ideological obedience, not thinking. Multinational conferences on justice become little more than echo chambers of posturing and finger-pointing. Nations condemn others while doing worse behind closed doors — and everyone knows. But the performance must go on.

It's not hypocrisy. It's theater. And every actor knows their lines.

We issue statements not for action, but for applause. We kneel for the camera. We tweet for peace while funding war. We brand ourselves as climate warriors while outsourcing emissions. We condemn injustice abroad while ignoring cruelty at home. The audience claps. The spotlight shifts. Nothing changes.

This isn't evolution. It isn't progress. It's the **old tribal machinery in high-definition**.

We haven't outgrown the mob. We've digitized it.
We haven't moved beyond public punishments. We've **gamified them**.
We haven't transcended performative virtue. We've **monetized it**.

The stage is bigger. The lines are smoother. The costumes are cleaner.

But the crowd is the same.
And they still want blood.

◆◆◆

Chapter 5

THE PATHOLOGY OF PROGRESS

"Progress is not evolution. It is an illusion, packaged in glass and steel."

The Modern Myth

We live under the comforting illusion that the world is getting better — that humanity is steadily ascending some moral staircase, shedding its primitive skin with each generation. We point to the skyscrapers, the smartphones, the clean suits and sleek glass towers, and we call it evolution. We've mistaken our inventions for evidence of enlightenment.

But progress is not the same as transformation. And history does not move in a straight line.

A better phone does not make a better soul.
A digital currency does not erase tribal instincts.
A satellite in orbit does not mean empathy on Earth.

The cities are smarter. The hearts are not.

Civilization has grown more complex, but the human operating system remains almost unchanged. We still crave status. We still fear differences. We still seek enemies. We still cheer for punishment. We've just become more efficient at hiding it — dressing our base impulses in the language of progress and pumping them through global networks at the speed of light.

We've built a world where cruelty travels faster, reaches farther, and is more easily monetized — and then we applaud ourselves for having "advanced."

Progress has become pathology. A story we tell ourselves to avoid reckoning with the truth: that we are not becoming better people. We are becoming better **performers**.

The modern myth of progress depends on one fragile assumption: that time alone improves humanity. That the passage of centuries must equal the rise of conscience. But there is no evidence for this. And worse — there is overwhelming evidence against it.

More people were murdered in the 20th century — the most "advanced" century in human history — than in any previous one. Auschwitz had engineers. Hiroshima had physicists. The Rwandan genocide was broadcast on television. Progress did not prevent these things. It enabled them.

We didn't outgrow barbarism.
We mechanized it.

And yet, we still tell ourselves the lie. That we are more tolerant. More just. More humane. That democracy has spread. That racism is ending. That war is in decline. But these are metrics of **presentation**, not transformation. It's not that we stopped being cruel. It's that we **stopped admitting it**.

We have PR campaigns instead of repentance.
We have hashtags instead of humility.
We have workshops instead of wisdom.

The pathology of progress is that it **doesn't cure the disease** — it convinces us we never had it. That all previous sins were the result of ignorance, and that we — we enlightened moderns — are the ones who finally got it right.

We speak of "being on the right side of history" as if history were a courtroom. As if history has a conscience. It doesn't. It's a mirror. And what it shows, again and again, is how easily people mistake comfort for goodness, advancement for character, and power for virtue.

The most dangerous people are not the ones who know they're capable of evil. The most dangerous are the ones who believe they've evolved beyond it.

They smile while they ruin you.
They retweet while they erase you.
They sleep soundly, because they've outsourced their conscience to the **idea of progress** — a myth they wear like armour.

But time does not sanctify.
Technology does not purify.
And the most "modern" societies can still burn people alive — they just do it digitally, and call it justice.

Historical Amnesia

If the myth of progress depends on the belief that we are getting better, then it also depends on something else:

Forgetting how bad we still are.

Our confidence in modern morality relies on historical amnesia — a collective forgetting of how recent, how local, and how *intimate* our barbarism really is.

The last lynching in the United States didn't happen in the 1800s. It happened in 1981.
South African apartheid — the systemic degradation of an entire race — ended in 1994.
The Rwandan genocide, where over 800,000 people were hacked to death with machetes by their neighbors, happened in 1994.

In 2002, reports of cannibalism emerged from the war-torn Congo.
In 2014, ISIS burned people alive — and **live-streamed it**.

This isn't ancient history.
This isn't myth.
This isn't tucked away in scrolls or stone tablets.

This is **within your lifetime**. Within your Wi-Fi era.
A few presidents ago. A few phones ago. A few headlines ago.

We don't remember — not because the cruelty ended — but because the *narrative of progress* requires us to forget. The mythology only works if we smooth out the timeline. So we bury recent horrors beneath a digital avalanche of TED Talks and virtue memes, and we call it healing.

But healing without memory is denial.
And denial is not growth — it's a trapdoor.

We marvel at our medical miracles. We've cured polio. We've mapped the genome. We've decoded the very instructions of life itself. We can split atoms and splice genes. We can rebuild hearts, clone sheep, and simulate consciousness.

But we still destroy reputations with rumors.
We still punish dissent with mob tactics.
We still kill — literally and figuratively — in the name of tribe, flag, or God.

We have drones that deliver emergency medicine.
And drones that deliver death to children in another country.
We have AI that designs beautiful images.
And AI that builds surveillance states.

We are gods with gadgets.
And infants with ethics.

Technology has outpaced psychology. Tools have evolved. **Souls have not**.

Progress gave us reach — but not restraint. It gave us speed — but not wisdom. It gave us voice — but not self-control. It put power in our hands before character formed in our hearts.

We live in a time where more people have access to education than at any point in history. Where information flows freely. Where encyclopedias live in our pockets. Where debates can span continents in seconds.

And yet — we are not more rational.
We are more reactive. More triggered. More ideologically possessed.

Children melt down over words.
Adults demand protection from opinions.
Students flee from disagreement as if it were violence.
Entire platforms erase satire, irony, and nuance to preserve a false sense of moral cleanliness.

We mistake emotional volatility for moral sensitivity.
We confuse feeling uncomfortable with being harmed.

And then we call it compassion.
We call it safety.
We call it justice.

But it's not justice.
It's **infantilization**, dressed in the costume of progress.

The adult mind is not disappearing — it's being delayed. Arrested in development. Sedated by comfort. Addicted to affirmation. Incapable of resilience.

We say we want truth — but we silence anything that stings.
We say we value courage — but we punish anyone who speaks without permission.
We say we are evolved — but we collapse into mobs the moment our illusions are touched.

We are building a society of moral toddlers with nuclear tools.
A civilization of **information without maturity**.
Emotion without discipline.
Volume without insight.

And we call it progress.
Because the buildings are taller.

The Illusion of Connectedness

We are more connected than ever. Wires span continents. Satellites bridge oceans. Voices bounce from one end of the Earth to the other in milliseconds. But for all our connection, we are disintegrating inside.

We report record levels of depression. We feel more isolated in cities of millions than villagers did in tribes of fifty. We medicate ourselves at historic rates — numbing not only pain, but awareness. We drown in noise and silence at the same time. Our minds flicker from feed to feed, screen to screen, distraction to distraction, while the body slumps, the soul flickers, and the purpose dissolves.

We do not speak anymore. We perform.
We do not relate. We brand.
We don't know how to be — only how to be *seen*.

This is not progress. This is a society overdosed on self-awareness and starved of self-control. We are flooded with mirrors but deprived of anchors. We know everything about everyone and nothing about ourselves.

And yet, the myth of progress persists. It *must* persist. Because to confront the truth would be unbearable.

To admit that our institutions are fragile.
That our compassion is conditional.
That our so-called virtue is circumstantial — a weather pattern of convenience.
That our morality is not a principle, but a performance that plays best when there's an audience and a reward.

We need to believe we're improving, not because it's true, but because the alternative is too terrifying: that we are clever children driving machines we do not understand — building systems we cannot emotionally sustain.

The myth helps us sleep. It whispers that the future will be brighter. That we are better than our ancestors. That we've transcended bloodlust, bias, and brutality. That "this time will be different." But history doesn't move in straight lines. And human nature doesn't upgrade with software.

We built the machine before we became adults. That is the essence of our predicament.

We've created technology that simulates godhood.
Machines that listen to every word.
Algorithms that anticipate thought and manipulate desire.
Artificial intelligence that can mimic creativity, emotion, even genius.

And yet — we still gossip like peasants.
We fear rejection like playground children.
We destroy reputations with whispers.
We mob together like villagers with pitchforks — only now the pitchfork is a trending hashtag.

We have built tools fit for gods — and handed them to creatures who still flinch at shadows and rejoice in collective punishment.

Our architecture is futuristic.
Our operating system is prehistoric.

We wear stainless steel, but we bleed like bronze.

And we call this freedom. But what we've created isn't agency — it's consumption disguised as choice.

You can choose your gender. Your pronouns. Your content feed. Your tribe. Your virtue signal of the week. But these choices don't root us. They scatter us. They disorient the psyche. They create identity overload — a thousand versions of "you" competing for validation.

We no longer belong to family, to culture, to sacred tradition — only to brands, slogans, influencer cults, and ephemeral tribes that dissolve the moment they become inconvenient.

We've traded rootedness for reach. Meaning for immediacy. Integrity for impressions.

And so now we are free — but anxious.
Powerful — but numb.
Endlessly expressive — and existentially hollow.

This is not progress.
It is psychological deregulation with a glowing user interface.

It is a spiritual collapse behind a filter.

We built cathedrals of steel, but we never matured the soul.
We walk through temples of data, but worship at altars of distraction.
We say we've evolved — but every scream, every banishment, every collapse of dialogue says otherwise.

Because at the heart of the myth of progress is a devastating truth:

We didn't outgrow the darkness.
We just put lights on it.

The Myth of Progress as a Weapon

In today's progressive culture, the phrase *"It's 2025"* isn't just a calendar reference. It's a moral bludgeon.

"It's 2025 — how can you still believe that?"
"It's 2025 — how can you question this?"
"It's 2025 — why aren't you using this language?"

As if time itself were a moral argument. As if the passage of years made dissent invalid. The assumption is that history always marches forward. That disagreement is regression. That tradition is inherently toxic, and doubt is a threat to the collective good.

But time doesn't think. Time doesn't care.

Slavery existed for millennia. Genocide has repeated like clockwork. Tyranny has been repackaged in every age, from robes to uniforms to suits. Time is not a moral force. It is a blank canvas onto which humanity projects its delusions — and perhaps the most dangerous delusion of all is the belief that progress is inevitable.

Because when that belief is questioned — when the myth is disturbed — the response is not reflection. It is rage.

We don't protect the myth because it's true.
We protect it because without it, we would have to face a truth we are terrified to confront:

We are not evolving.
We are circling.
We are repeating ourselves with better marketing.

Nowhere is this pathology more visible than in the most privileged corners of the modern world — in air-conditioned cities, filled with abundance, safety, and convenience — where people crumble under the weight of a tweet, dissolve at the sound of an opposing view, and label discomfort as trauma.

We are told this is because we're more enlightened. More sensitive. More evolved.

But what if it's the opposite?

What if this fragility isn't the mark of moral progress, but **the symptom of spiritual atrophy**?
What if the absence of hardship hasn't made us gentle — but made us hollow?

We do not endure suffering, so we invent it.
We do not fight wars, so we simulate them on social media.
We do not face death, so we create outrage to feel alive.

We cry over Netflix dramas but ignore real genocide.
We cancel comedians while tolerating corruption.
We panic over misused pronouns but scroll past images of actual violence.

This is not compassion.
This is **moral displacement** — fury in the wrong direction, sensitivity without substance, pain without purpose.

We mistake our outrage for ethics. Our performance for principle. Our fragility for evolution.

But the more we worship comfort, the more allergic we become to reality. The myth of progress — once meant to inspire — has become a mask for decay. It conceals the fact that we are spiritually malnourished, morally confused, and addicted to appearances.

We think we're advanced because we stopped believing in hell.
But we've created new ones: isolation, anxiety, chronic loneliness, attention collapse, identity confusion.
We built cathedrals of science, but forgot that science has no values.
We optimized every second of the day, but forgot what we're optimizing for.
We programmed morality into machines, but never programmed it into ourselves.

We idolize progress — but never ask:
Progress toward what?
At what cost?

This is the pathology of progress:

A civilization that believes it is immune to collapse,
A culture that confuses conformity with character,
A generation that recites slogans but cannot sit in silence,
A moral system so brittle, so performative, it shatters under dissent. We don't need more data.
We don't need better therapy.
We don't need another upgrade, another app, another framework.

We need the courage to ask:
Are we truly better?
Or are we just better at pretending?

Case Study: Mao's Agricultural Catastrophe

When truth threatens power, truth is outlawed.

In the late 1950s and 60s, under Mao Zedong's **Great Leap Forward**, Chinese agriculture was restructured not by science — but by ideology. Peasants were ordered to follow **politicized farming methods** like deep plowing and close planting, based on unproven theories Mao believed reflected Communist values of collectivism and struggle.

Local officials, desperate to appear loyal, **falsified crop yields**, destroyed dissenting reports, and punished those who questioned the methods. Scientists who warned of disaster were denounced as "reactionaries." Starvation was blamed on "counter-revolutionaries," not the policies that caused it.

The result?
Tens of millions of people died in what became the worst famine in recorded history.

There was no progress.
Just **performative obedience** masquerading as vision.
And behind every smiling propaganda poster stood a grave dug by ideology.

Chapter 6

THE RETURN OF THE SACRED ENEMY

"Without a devil, the tribe has no story."

The Enemy Is Sacred

"You are not righteous… until someone else is evil."

Every society has its gods. But no society survives without its devils.

We speak today of tolerance, of coexistence, of universal morality. But scratch the surface — peel back the slogans and institutional gloss — and you will find something ancient pulsing underneath: the need for an enemy. A figure to blame. A shadow to fear. A vessel into which we can pour all our anxiety, confusion, and hidden violence.

In every ancient culture, goodness was never defined universally.
It was tribal.
Obedience was virtue.
Loyalty was righteousness.
And betrayal — even the quiet kind — was sin.

You were moral only in relation to the group.
You were just only in contrast to the enemy.

And always — *always* — there was a sacred enemy. Not just someone to defeat, but someone whose existence was **necessary** for the group to remain whole.

- For early Christians, it was the heretic — the one who poisoned doctrine.
- For the Inquisition, the witch — the woman who corrupted purity.
- For Stalinists, the kulak — the farmer who owned too much.
- For Maoists, the landlord — the reminder of class shame.
- For jihadists, the infidel — the nonbeliever who desecrated divine order.

- For fascists, the subversive — the one who questioned the national body.

These weren't just enemies. They were **theological figures**, dressed in modern costumes. Their destruction wasn't political — it was ritual. Their erasure wasn't sad — it was sacred.

Because to destroy the enemy was to cleanse the self.
To burn the heretic was to prove your own faith.
To hang the traitor was to renew your belonging.

The sacred enemy is the mirror image of the tribe — not just what it opposes, but what it fears becoming.
They must be hated, not simply because they are different — but because they once *could* have been us.
Their proximity is the threat. Their humanity is the danger.

We don't burn monsters. We burn **reflections**.

And in every era, a new mask is placed on the same face.

The sacred enemy isn't born. **They are chosen.** Selected, not for their deeds, but for what they symbolize — what they allow the group to *offload*.

This is the psychology of scapegoating — one of the oldest survival mechanisms in the human mind. When anxiety surges, when cohesion cracks, when a tribe or a nation or an ideology feels unstable, it instinctively seeks to restore order through **sacrifice**.

Not introspection.
Not dialogue.
Sacrifice.

Anthropologist René Girard called this the **mimetic cycle** — where human desire, rivalry, and fear build tension within a group until it finds release through the **identification and elimination of a scapegoat**. The victim may be guilty. But they don't need to be. Their function is not justice — it is *purification*.

The scapegoat unifies the tribe.
They take the sins of the many — real or imagined — and concentrate them into one body.
And when that body is expelled, punished, burned, erased — the tribe breathes again.
The chaos dissipates.
The ritual is complete.

It's not hard to see why this works. Blame is easier than complexity. Punishment is faster than healing. And the elimination of *one* feels more manageable than the reckoning of *all*.

But the terrifying power of scapegoating lies not in its brutality — but in how **good it feels**.

There is an almost sacred relief that descends when the group agrees: *"That's the one."*
The tension lifts. The doubt vanishes. Certainty returns.
And righteousness becomes collective, electric, even euphoric.

This is why mobs form with lightning speed.
Why outrage spreads faster than truth.
Why silence feels like complicity — and why questioning the narrative makes *you* suspect.

Because once the scapegoat has been named, **hesitation becomes heresy**.

Even more disturbing is how often scapegoats are chosen from *within*.
The outsider is threatening — but it's the insider-turned-traitor who truly terrifies.
The ex-believer. The moderate. The one who speaks too softly when everyone else is shouting.

They must be cast out. Not just to protect the tribe — but to **reaffirm it**.

This is why modern cancel culture feels less like justice and more like an exorcism.
Why whistleblowers are crushed.
Why internal dissenters are labeled as threats, not assets.
Why the "fallen ally" is punished harder than the original enemy.

Because once you've seen the inner workings of the tribe, and you still deviate — you are no longer mistaken.
You are **unclean**.

Scapegoating isn't just a failure of justice. It's a failure of courage.

It's the coward's substitute for introspection.
It's what people do when their worldview can't bear contradiction.
It's how civilizations rot — not through war, but through the slow decay of honesty.

And in our age, it's evolved.

We no longer tie people to poles.
We tie them to narratives.
We don't stone them in the square.
We erase them from feeds.
We don't hear their defense.
We *edit* it, reframe it, and bury it in a scrollable graveyard of algorithms and memes.

But make no mistake — the scapegoat still dies.

Not in body, but in reputation.
Not in court, but in public sentiment.
Not through proof, but through momentum.

But scapegoating doesn't just happen in volatile regimes or forgotten history books. It is alive in the bloodstream of modernity — updated, secularized, and algorithmically accelerated.

God May Be Dead, But the Devil Thrives

We tell ourselves we live in a secular age — that we've outgrown myth and moral absolutism. Church attendance is down. Sacred texts are mocked. The vocabulary of original sin has been replaced by sociology and hashtags. But our instincts haven't gone anywhere. The stage changed — the ritual did not.

Because we still crave moral drama.
We still need heroes.
We still demand villains.
We still yearn for purity, and we still rage for blood.

So we consecrate new devils — secular icons of everything we must destroy to prove that we are good.
- The capitalist becomes the earth's executioner.
- The anti-vaxxer becomes a murderer of children.
- The straight white male becomes the living avatar of structural sin.
- The Zionist becomes the modern colonizer with blood on his hands.
- The woke progressive becomes a Maoist cultist plotting civilizational collapse.

These are no longer political disagreements.
They are **theological conflicts** — full of sacred language, apocalyptic stakes, and unyielding righteousness.

We do not debate these people.
We excommunicate them.
We do not see opponents.
We see *apostates* — heretics whose very presence threatens the coherence of the tribe.

And this is the final, brutal truth:
The sacred enemy is not hated because of what they've done.
They are hated because **we need them**.

Without the enemy, the tribe's identity collapses.
Without the enemy, there is no clarity — only doubt.
Without the enemy, there is no moral high ground — only complexity.

The sacred enemy provides structure. Urgency. Meaning.

- If racism begins to lessen, we widen its definition to keep it alive.
- If oppression fades, we invent new hierarchies of harm.
- If injustice subsides, we label discomfort as violence.
- If there is no enemy to fight, we turn on our own until one is found.

Because the rituals must continue.
Because the outrage must have a target.
Because the tribe without a devil is a tribe without cohesion.

The sacred enemy is the glue.
And so, if they no longer exist — they will be imagined.
They will be summoned.
And when that fails, they will be manufactured.

This is not evolution.
This is liturgy without God.
This is religious fervor poured into secular molds.
And the result is a culture that masquerades as progress, but survives through **perpetual purification**.

The Enemy Must Burn

The sacred enemy cannot simply disappear.
They must be punished — publicly, dramatically, sacrificially.

The mob doesn't just want dissent to end.
It wants to **watch** it end.
It wants to feel righteous in the destruction.
It wants to feel **cleansed** by the spectacle.

So we don't just cancel.
We fire.
We shame.
We digitally stone, socially exile, economically destroy — not in the pursuit of justice, but as a **performance of belonging**.

The act isn't about truth.
It's about solidarity.
It's how the tribe reaffirms itself — through **ritual violence**.

This is no different than the crowd at the gallows.
Or the villagers gathered to burn the witch.
Or the revolutionary council signing the death warrant of yesterday's hero.

It is not policy.
It is **blood magic** — dressed in progressive language and hashtags.

And the more enlightened a society *believes* itself to be, the more violently it must purge the impure — to maintain the illusion that it is *still evolving*. This is how moral cleanliness becomes indistinguishable from ideological cannibalism.

Girard described this as the deep structure of civilization — **scapegoating** not as an exception, but as foundation.

Every tribe, movement, and culture builds tension: fear, doubt, resentment, insecurity. When the pressure becomes unbearable, introspection would be healthy. But **violence is easier**. And so the group looks outward. It finds someone close. Someone slightly different. Someone formerly within — now just far enough to blame.

The scapegoat is rarely guilty.
They are just **available**.

And so the ritual begins:

"It's not our fault — it's *his* fault."
"We didn't fail — *she* betrayed us."
"We're not cruel — *they* deserved it."

The destruction of the scapegoat **restores order**.
It releases pressure.
It reaffirms belief.
It lets the tribe exhale.

And the more sacred the tribe believes itself to be — the more **savage** the purge must be to preserve its illusion.

This is why revolutions eat their children.
Why movements devour their founders.
Why "safe spaces" implode into silencing rituals.

Why progressive circles turn inwards, slicing themselves into ever-narrower purity hierarchies.

Because once the system requires purity to survive, **no one is safe**.
Everyone becomes a potential threat.
And the violence doesn't stop. It feeds.

The scapegoat is not a **glitch** in the system.
The scapegoat **is the system** — rebranded as accountability, justice, liberation.

But underneath the hashtags and policies, the architecture is the same:
Choose someone. Make them dirty. Destroy them. And feel whole again.

Case Study: Zionism as the Modern Scapegoat

In the aftermath of the October 7, 2023 attacks — where Israeli civilians were massacred in their homes, streets, and at a music festival — the world responded.
Not with clarity. Not with balance. But with a **ritual purge**.
Yes, Hamas was briefly condemned. But within days, the narrative shifted — not toward nuanced critique, but toward **total moral inversion**:

- Israel was no longer defending itself — it was now the villain.
- Zionism was no longer nationalism — it became **a codeword for genocide**.
- Jews across the world — many of them unaffiliated with Israel — became targets, both literally and symbolically.

What was happening?
The world — overwhelmed by complexity, trauma, and moral tension — **needed a scapegoat**.

- The Palestinians were framed exclusively as victims — innocent, voiceless, righteous.

- The Israelis were reimagined as colonizers, aggressors, even Nazis — regardless of historical truth.

It didn't matter that:

- Israel is smaller than New Jersey.
- It was attacked unprovoked.
- It pulled out of Gaza in 2005.
- It contains 2 million Arab citizens with voting rights.

Facts were irrelevant.
The ritual demanded a villain.

And the term *"Zionist"* became a **totemic curse word** — used not to critique policy, but to dehumanize an identity:
"Zionist" became interchangeable with "subhuman," "aggressor," "murderer."
At Harvard, Columbia, Oxford — students and faculty publicly justified the killing of civilians.
On social media, **"Zionists" were openly called rats, pigs, and disease**.
In Europe, synagogues were defaced — not because of what Israel did, but because **a scapegoat had been chosen.**
This wasn't activism. It wasn't resistance.
It was **a purification ritual**, written in blood and posture.

Why Zionism Became the Perfect Scapegoat

1. **It is symbolically powerful** — tied to land, ethnicity, history, and religion.
2. **It is globally visible** — thanks to Western media and cultural influence.
3. **It represents contradiction** — a people who were once victims, now seen as strong.

4. **It offers a "safe" way to revive old hatreds** —
anti-Semitism under a new, fashionable name.

And once the scapegoat is identified, the system demands **total participation**:

- Silence becomes complicity
- Nuance becomes betrayal
- Empathy becomes treason

The ritual is not complete until the tribe feels unified again.
Until the scapegoat is **destroyed**, and the illusion of moral purity is restored. The sacred enemy is not an ancient relic. It is alive, rebranded, and mass-produced in schools, governments, media, and minds. We don't worship gods. We worship moral identity.

And **we sacrifice human beings to protect that worship**. You are not allowed to be complex. You are not allowed to be both good and flawed. You are either a priest — or you are the sacrifice.

Are "good people" real — or are they just evolutionary glitches in a species hardwired for self-interest, tribalism, and cruelty?

Chapter 7

EXCEPTIONS OR EXCUSES?

"We praise saints because we know how rare they are."

The Myth of the Good Person

We grow up believing in the existence of good people.

Not just people who do good things — but good people as a category.

As an identity.
Heroes. Humanitarians. Parents. Teachers. Activists. Clergy. The moral backbone of society.

We are taught that goodness lives in character — a stable trait, reinforced by upbringing, rewarded by community, honored in history. The stories we consume reflect this faith: the selfless neighbor, the incorruptible leader, the brave soul who stands up while others look away.

But what if that belief is a story we tell to comfort ourselves?

Because when you look closely — past the curated posts, the heartfelt speeches, the charitable headlines — you find something else.
Something darker.
Something consistent.

- The philanthropist dodging taxes while giving to the poor.
- The activist exploiting interns behind closed doors.
- The priest silencing victims in the name of reputation.
- The psychologist grooming patients under the guise of healing.
- The family man erupting in private, smiling in public.

Are these outliers?
Or are they the norm — temporarily restrained by optics, culture, or fear of exposure?

Maybe goodness is not a character trait.
Maybe it's a **condition** — a performance we maintain when the incentives align.

Maybe "good" isn't who you are.
Maybe it's who you appear to be — until stress, power, fear, or anonymity reveals something else.

Are Morally Good People Just Mutations?

Biology may offer a brutal answer.

There's a term in neuroscience: **pro-social outlier**.
These are people who, without threat of punishment or hope for reward, consistently act with integrity. They:

- Return the wallet, even when no one would notice.
- Speak truth to power, even when it costs them everything.
- Defend the outcast, even when it makes them hated.
- Control their rage, even when it's justified.
- Feel guilt, even when no one is watching.

MRI scans show these individuals have unusually high integration between the **prefrontal cortex** (responsible for reason, restraint, and future thinking) and the **limbic system** (which governs emotion and impulse).
In other words: they're neurologically wired to resist tribalism, vengeance, and self-interest.

But they are rare.

Very rare.

Most of us are:
- Kind when convenient
- Brave when it earns applause
- Generous when it serves our image
- Honest until the stakes rise
- Peaceful until we're humiliated
- Forgiving until it's personal

So maybe the right question isn't:
"Why are so many people bad?"

Maybe it's:
"Why are the few who are good — good at all?"

Goodness Without Witness

The real test of character isn't what you say on social media.
It's what you do when **no one will ever know**.
- Do you help the weak when there's no credit?
- Do you tell the truth when it costs you?
- Do you choose mercy over vengeance when no one would blame you for retaliation?
- Do you return what isn't yours — even when it would solve your problems?

If the answer is no — then maybe you're not *good*.
Maybe you're **trained**.

Trained by reward and punishment.
Trained by applause and shame.
Trained by scripts, not principles.

And if that's true, then what are all our laws, our systems, our institutions?
Not sanctuaries of morality — but **cages** to hold back the beast.

Because when the lights go out, when the crowd disperses, when the consequences disappear —
most people don't rise.
They **revert**.

We are not angels corrupted by circumstance.
We are animals conditioned by structure.
And "goodness," for most, is not a state of being — but a **strategy** for social survival.

The Outlier: Witold Pilecki, The Man Who Entered Hell Voluntarily

During World War II, in Nazi-occupied Poland, most people tried to stay invisible. To survive. To protect their families.
But **Witold Pilecki** did something so incomprehensibly selfless,
historians still struggle to categorize it.
He volunteered to be captured and sent to Auschwitz.
Not to escape. Not to infiltrate and destroy it.
But to **gather intelligence**, build resistance from inside, and **alert the world to the horrors occurring within.**
He starved. He was beaten. He witnessed thousands die.
He smuggled reports out. No one believed him.
He eventually escaped — and then re-entered active resistance against the Nazis.
After the war, he was **executed by the communists** for being a "traitor."

Pilecki gained nothing.
No medals. No applause. No redemption arc.
Only pain, isolation, and death.
But he did the right thing.
Not because it was safe.
Not because it was rewarded.
But because it was right.
This is what moral outliers look like.
They do good when everyone else chooses safety, silence, or complicity.

False Positives: Institutional Goodness is Often a Costume

In contrast, most of what we call "good" behavior today is not moral. It's **incentivized compliance**.

- The executive signs a diversity pledge because it protects his career.
- The politician visits a shelter for the photo op.
- The celebrity cries for a cause they researched five minutes ago.
- The student repeats approved talking points to avoid being labeled.
- The employee donates because the company announced who gave the most.

None of this is *bad*.
But it's not goodness.
It's social navigation.

Institutions — schools, companies, media, governments — don't reward ethics.
They reward:
- Predictability
- Loyalty
- Branding
- Obedience

In these systems:
- Speaking truth becomes "risk."
- Asking questions becomes "hostility."
- Refusing ritual becomes "harm."
- Independent thought becomes "a problem."

So people perform goodness instead of practicing it.
They signal morality instead of embodying it.
And because the performance is rewarded, they convince themselves:

"I must be a good person. Look how I'm being applauded."

But the applause is for **compliance**, not courage.
For fluency in the moral dialect, not fluency in actual conscience.

These are **false positives** of virtue — outputs that look moral but are generated entirely by pressure and pattern recognition.
Like a deepfake of the soul, they mimic empathy without feeling it, quote values without living them, and parrot justice while avoiding the cost of it.

This is how institutions protect their image while ignoring their rot.
They create elaborate systems of moral optics — DEI statements, vision boards, awareness weeks — all of which allow them to simulate accountability without confronting abuse, corruption, or ethical decay.

And worse, they **reward the best performers** — the most polished mask-wearers — as if those closest to the script are closest to integrity.

Over time, people begin to **associate approval with goodness**, and silence their internal compass.
The reward system rewires them.
Not toward deeper reflection — but toward **moral automation**.

Because when obedience becomes the path to praise, courage becomes a liability.
And in such a world, the truly ethical person is not promoted — they are punished.

When Conscience Becomes a Threat

True morality — practiced, principled, and consistent — is not always welcome in modern institutions. In fact, it is often treated as a **liability**.

Why?

Because genuine moral clarity refuses to bend when the rules demand silence.
Because real conscience doesn't clock in and out according to quarterly targets or trending causes.
Because it **disrupts**.

The ethical outlier — the one who refuses to lie, who refuses to ignore harm, who questions the slogans and critiques the rituals — is rarely rewarded.
More often, they are:
- Sidelined
- Labeled "difficult"
- Accused of lacking "team spirit"
- Quietly removed from promotion lists

- Or ousted altogether under the guise of "culture fit"

Because in performance-based systems, **alignment is safer than integrity**.
Someone who actually follows their conscience cannot be controlled.
And systems built on optics cannot afford **unmanaged truth**.

This is why whistleblowers are punished.
Why internal critics are silenced.
Why those who speak for the abused are often discarded, while those who protect the institution are promoted.

True morality **exposes the fraud**.
It makes the system uncomfortable.
And in return, the system often turns on the moral outlier — **not because they are wrong**, but because they are **dangerous** to the illusion.

Case Study: The Fall of "America's Dad"

For decades, Bill Cosby was held up as a model of moral uprightness. He was more than a comedian — he was a **cultural symbol**.

- A Black man who "transcended race"
- A father figure who preached family values
- A role model who championed education, discipline, and decency
- A speaker who chastised young people for failing to live up to standards of respectability

He was celebrated, awarded, and trusted — not just because of his talent, but because of his **image**.

An image polished by institutions that rewarded him with honorary degrees, corporate deals, and national platforms.

But behind the carefully constructed mask was something else.
Dozens of women eventually came forward with horrifying stories of rape, drugging, manipulation, and coercion — accusations that spanned decades and were systematically ignored or buried.

Why?

Because Cosby's image served a purpose.
He was profitable.
He was politically useful.
He was the **perfect symbol** for a society eager to believe in moral progress without doing the hard work of moral scrutiny.

And so the system protected him — until the flood could no longer be dammed.
Until the myth collapsed under its own weight.
And suddenly, the man who built a career on judgment was exposed as **morally bankrupt**.

His case is not just about one man.
It is a cautionary tale about how easily we are fooled by the performance of virtue.
How institutions — schools, networks, corporations, even courts — will tolerate monstrous behavior as long as it comes wrapped in the right **story**.

Because in the end, the lie that someone *is good* is often easier to sell than the truth that goodness must be **proven, reproven,** and **practiced** — even when no one is watching.

The Illusion Must Be Maintained

If moral goodness is this rare — if pro-social outliers are exceptions, not the rule — then why does society still believe in "good people"?

Why do we need this myth so badly?

Because without it, the mirror becomes unbearable.

We need to believe in decency — even if we have to fake it.
We need to believe in conscience — even if we outsource it to algorithms, HR policies, or social media trends.
We need to believe that our institutions are filled with people doing the right thing — not people performing the right moves to keep their jobs, their image, or their status.

So we manufacture goodness the way we manufacture celebrities.
We **assign it**.
We brand it.
We reward its costume, not its content.

A priest in robes.
A teacher in a blazer.
A CEO on stage.
A student in the "right" shirt, saying the "right" words.
A parent who makes the neighbours nod in approval.
A therapist with awards.
A politician holding a child.

These become our proxies for goodness.
We project virtue onto the uniform, not the person.

Because it's easier.
It's cleaner.
It allows us to sleep.

And the moment the mask cracks — the moment the truth leaks out — we don't re-examine the system.
We just replace the actor.
We recast the role.
We pretend the story still works.

We say, "That wasn't a good person after all."
We never say, "Maybe there are no truly good people."
*Because that admission is **terrifying**.*

If goodness is that rare — if it is not a default but a mutation — then what are we?
What are *you*?

Would you protect the innocent if no one ever found out?
Would you return the money if it meant your family went hungry?
Would you refuse to lie, even if it cost you your career?
Would you defend the hated — not the misunderstood — but the truly loathed, if you knew they were innocent?

Would you?

Most wouldn't.
Not because they're evil.
But because they are *normal*.
Conditioned.
Reactive.
Fearful.
Tribal.

That is the human baseline.
That is why the world looks the way it does.
That is why peace collapses, justice cracks, and cruelty returns again and again, wrapped in new slogans and new justifications.

We say, "Be a good person."
But we don't mean it.

We mean: **Perform goodness.**
Signal loyalty.
Obey the script.
And never threaten the myth.

Because if we questioned it too deeply — if we truly admitted how rare real moral courage is — we would have to rebuild everything:

- Our laws
- Our heroes
- Our education
- Our parenting
- Our stories
- Our self-image

And most terrifying of all — we would have to admit:
The monsters we fear aren't hiding in the dark.
They're sitting beside us.
Sometimes, they are us.

That is why the illusion of goodness is not just preserved.
It is **sacred**.

We don't need it to be true.
We just need it to be *believable*.

And so, we carry on — calling ourselves moral, wearing our masks, clapping for others in costume — while the few truly good people walk among us like ghosts.

Not praised.
Not understood.

Just quietly resisting the tide…
and proving, by their very existence, how few of us actually deserve the title: **good**.

Chapter 8

BLOOD IS CONDITIONAL

"Even a parent will disown the child to protect the tribe."

The Myth of Unconditional Love

We are raised on a promise so sacred it is almost mythological:

A parent's love is unconditional.
Family is forever.
Blood is thicker than water.

But reality often tells a much colder truth.

Because the same mouths that whisper, *"I'll always love you,"* are sometimes the first to go silent when a child strays from the script.
Mothers stop answering the phone.
Fathers close the door.
The tribal walls close in.

And for what?

Children are disowned for being gay.
For dating outside the race.
For getting pregnant.
For getting arrested.
For leaving the faith.
For speaking the truth.
For bringing "shame."

It's not because they became unlovable.
It's because the parent became afraid — of losing social status, of being judged, of being tainted by association.
What we call "unconditional love" is, all too often, a **conditional**

contract — one built on the child's alignment with the tribe's moral expectations.

The moment the child becomes a mirror of discomfort, a threat to image, or a crack in the tribe's façade, the contract is revoked.

This is not rare.
It is ancient.
It is **wired into the human psyche**.

Because when a child violates the moral framework of the family — religiously, politically, sexually, socially — the parent doesn't just face disappointment.
They face a **moral identity crisis**:

> "Do I protect my child — or protect my place in the tribe?"
> "Do I defend my son — or defend my reputation?"
> "Do I stand beside my daughter — or stand with my community?"

Most choose the latter.
Not because they're monsters.
But because **belonging is survival**, and **shame is contagious**.

The deepest human fear isn't being wrong — it's **being seen as wrong by others**.
So they cut ties.
They turn their backs.
They rewrite the story to protect themselves.

And in that moment, even the primal bond of parenthood can be severed.

From an evolutionary perspective, it's horrifyingly logical.
We are wired to protect our offspring — but only when they enhance the

group's chance of survival.
When a child becomes:

- Too deviant
- Too outspoken
- Too weak
- Too likely to attract punishment or exile

Abandonment becomes a **tribal survival strategy**.
It is not "evil."
It is **instinct** — dressed in the language of disappointment, righteousness, or "tough love."

We protect our children…
But only as long as they stay inside the lines.

Once they cross them — once they violate the tribe's emotional hygiene — they are often no longer sons or daughters.
They are **liabilities**.

And suddenly, "unconditional love" comes with **fine print**.

Case Study: Turning In Your Own

In the days following the January 6th U.S. Capitol riot, a number of American parents called the FBI to report their own children.

- In one case, a mother turned in her son after seeing him in news footage.
- She said she did it "because it was the right thing to do."
- Others followed suit — some reportedly in tears, others proud of their decision.

But behind the headlines was something more primal:
They feared being seen as enablers. As traitors. As bad parents.
And in a world where **moral alignment matters more than blood**, they chose the tribe.
These parents weren't cruel.
They were performing **social redemption through sacrifice**.

Religious Excommunication of Children

Across cultures and religions, the child who deviates is not merely corrected — they are often exiled.

- Christian parents excommunicate children who renounce the faith.
- Muslim families disown daughters for dating outside the religion.
- Orthodox Jews mourn their apostate sons and daughters as if they had died — sitting *shiva* not for a corpse, but for a living betrayal.

These are not isolated incidents.
They are not "extreme cases."
They are **institutionalized rituals of disavowal**, practiced in pews, temples, mosques, and living rooms alike.

They send a singular, unmistakable message:

> "You are loved — but only if you reflect what we believe."
> "You are family — but only as long as you do not dishonour us."

In these worlds, **love is not a lifeline**.
It is a **mirror** — and the moment it reflects dissent, it is shattered.

But not all abandonment is loud.
Not all rejection comes in shouting matches or exile ceremonies.

Sometimes, the parent just… stops speaking.
Stops defending.
Stops protecting.

They do not scream.
They disappear.

They shrink into the shadows when the child is accused.
They remain silent when the child is mocked, canceled, disowned by others.
They withdraw — subtly, but unmistakably — as if the distance will **cleanse their own name**.

This is not hatred.
It is fear disguised as integrity.

It is the quietest form of betrayal:

> "If I act like I don't know them, maybe I'll be spared."

These parents are not monsters.
They are **performers** — caught in the spotlight of social morality, and desperate not to be next.

Because in modern society, being a "good parent" is no longer judged by how you **care for your child**, but how you **appear to care**.

We romanticize the image of the good parent:
- The one who protects without question
- Who loves without condition
- Who stands beside their child through fire and flood

But in reality, a "good parent" is increasingly defined by their **public alignment with moral trends**.

They are watched.
They are judged.
They are ranked in whispers and hashtags.

So when their child misbehaves, falters, or sins in the eyes of the tribe, the parent faces a choice that no myth prepares them for:

> "Will you disown your child to restore your image?"

Many do.
Not out of cruelty — but out of a desperate need to **preserve their performance of goodness**.

Because in today's moral economy, loyalty to one's child can be interpreted as *agreement* with their failure.
And the crowd doesn't care about love.
The crowd cares about **optics**.

And so, even the sacred bond — the primal thread between parent and child — becomes a **theater of sacrifice**, where silence is applause, distance is proof, and love is overwritten by the need to survive the moral mob.

The Child as Moral Mirror

To many parents, a child is not an individual. A child is a mirror — polished, shaped, and displayed for the world to reflect back their virtue, their legacy, their sacrifice, their name. If the reflection gleams, the parent is proud. If the reflection cracks, the parent panics.

If the child becomes a doctor, the parent posts about it. If the child becomes an addict, the parent hides it. If the child comes out as gay, the parent rewrites their version of family history. If the child is canceled, the parent cuts ties to avoid guilt by association.

Why? Because in the fragile psychology of a reputation-obsessed society, the child is not a human being. The child is an extension of the tribe's self-image. And any deviation from the script becomes a threat to the myth. "You didn't just make a mistake. You made *me* look bad. And for that… you must be erased."

This isn't new. It is ancient. In tribal history, embarrassment was danger. To shame the tribe was to endanger its place in the hierarchy. And the response was swift: exile, disownment, purification by silence. We've kept the ritual. We've just updated the language. Today, "You have shamed us" becomes: "You've left me no choice." "This isn't how I raised you." "Until you change, don't contact me." But the core mechanism remains the same: punish the reflection to protect the mirror.

Disownment is not a backwoods phenomenon. It thrives in PTA groups, church halls, corporate LinkedIn feeds, and suburban living rooms.

A 16-year-old gymnast, trained since childhood, tears her ACL before Olympic qualifiers. Her father — who filmed every practice and tattooed her name beneath Olympic rings — stops speaking to her. Not because she failed. But because she ruined the narrative. The fairy tale was his. Her injury was a betrayal of it.

A college student is caught plagiarizing a paper. The university issues a minor disciplinary warning. Her mother posts on Facebook — not to support her, but to denounce her. "I raised my daughter to know right from wrong. Until she takes accountability, I can't support her choices." Translation: "Don't cancel me with her."

A son renounces his evangelical faith and quietly leaves the church. At the next Sunday service, the father stands before the congregation and announces, "My son is spiritually dead." Not a conversation. A ritual execution — clean, public, irreversible.

None of these children committed crimes. They didn't harm others. They harmed a myth. They dented the parent's reflection. And for that, they were cut out like tumours.

The disowned child isn't confused by morality. They're confused by the conditions of love. "I thought I was your son." "I thought love meant protection." "So it was never about who I was — it was about what I gave you." And in that moment, love reveals itself not as sanctuary, but as currency. A currency bound to performance, image, and obedience. Spend it wrong — and it's gone.

You are no longer a son. No longer a daughter. You are a moral liability.

In families obsessed with optics, love is never unconditional. It is a contract. It is a brand. And the child is expected to protect that brand at all costs — or be erased from the billboard.

The Ritual of Redemptive Abandonment

Disowning a child is rarely framed as cruelty. It is often framed as moral courage. A parent doesn't say, "I gave up on my son." They say, "I had to make a hard choice." They don't say, "I abandoned my daughter." They say, "She left me no option." This is not confession. This is performance. And it is applauded — not just in quiet gossip, but sometimes publicly. Because in a society built on optics, even betrayal can be branded as virtue.

The act of casting out your own flesh becomes a kind of redemptive ritual. It signals alignment with the tribe. It reassures the group: "I am not like them. I chose principle over blood." It is the modern equivalent of burning your own heretic child on the altar to prove loyalty to the gods. "Look how far I'm willing to go," says the parent. "Even my own child isn't safe from my values." But these values are not moral. They are tribal. They are survival strategies dressed in righteousness.

This is the same pattern we've seen in every culture across time: cast out the unclean to restore balance. The leper. The apostate. The disobedient son. The daughter who fell from grace. The scapegoat must be sacrificed, even when that scapegoat is your own child. Because the tribe must be appeased. And in this framework, punishment becomes penance — and abandonment becomes a badge of honor.

But love — real love — is not tested in the child's success. Anyone can love a golden child. It is easy to love a trophy. It is easy to boast about the straight-A student, the gifted athlete, the obedient believer. That is not love. That is pride in disguise.

Love is tested when the child collapses. When the child deviates. When the child becomes an embarrassment. When they fail, fall, fracture — and stop being a mirror you're proud of. That is when the truth of love is revealed.

And most people fail that test.

Not because they are bad parents. But because love, as we like to describe it — as pure, unconditional, noble — is a myth. It is not a natural state. It is not hardwired. Love is not what we think it is.

Love, in most cases, is conditional. It is fragile. It is tribal. It is reputational. It is a contract based on mutual performance: You behave how I need you to — and I give you affection. Break the terms, and the warmth goes cold. For many, this is unconscious. But it is no less real.

This is why so many parents, when their children disappoint them, turn not to conversation — but to condemnation. Not to compassion — but to distance. They do not lean in. They step away. Because to stay close to the deviant child is to risk guilt by proximity. And the tribe does not tolerate proximity to deviance.

So love becomes not a sanctuary, but a scoreboard. Fail the wrong way, and the tally resets. And what once felt like home becomes a courtroom.

We must stop telling children that love is unconditional when what we actually model is performance-based approval. We must stop pretending that family loyalty is eternal when we weaponize it the moment reputation is at risk. And we must stop pretending that abandonment is courage.

Because the truth is brutal: most people do not love their children — they love the *idea* of their children. And when that idea is shattered, what's left is not love. What's left is instinct. And instinct only protects what the tribe will praise.

When Love Becomes a Mirror of Guilt

A child does not process rejection with reason. They do not say: "My parent was weak." "My parent gave in to pressure." "My parent feared judgment." They say: "It's me. I'm the problem." "If the one who created me can't love me… something inside me must be unlovable." This is not logic. This is biology.

From infancy, the child's survival depends on parental attachment. When that bond is severed — especially not for violence, but for nonconformity — the child's nervous system codes it as a threat: I did something wrong. I am something wrong. The child does not grieve the parent. They grieve the illusion that they were safe to be themselves. And what replaces that illusion is a corrosive identity built around shame — not for what was done, but for who they are.

When a parent disowns a child — explicitly or silently — the impact isn't situational. It's existential. A daughter disowned for her sexuality doesn't just feel grief. She begins to question if love itself is safe. A son turned away for a moral failure doesn't just feel guilt. He feels cursed — stained in a way no apology can cleanse. A child rejected for challenging religion, tradition, or political identity doesn't feel free.

They feel contaminated — as though they brought shame not just to the family, but to existence. This isn't guilt. This is shame alchemy — where an action becomes a reflection of self-worth. Shame becomes a skin. It can't be washed off. It isn't about what happened. It becomes: "Who I am must be wrong." "Otherwise, they would've stayed."

Children who are emotionally or publicly abandoned rarely "move on."

They adapt.

They mutate.

They perform survival.

Perfectionism develops as a trauma reflex — "Maybe if I'm perfect, I'll be loved again." People-pleasing becomes safety — "If I upset anyone, I might lose them too." Emotional dissociation grows — "I'll never be that vulnerable again."

Relationships become rehearsals of rejection — attracting those who confirm the belief: You are hard to love. Even in adulthood, the echo persists: "If my own mother gave up on me, why would anyone else stay?" "If my father could erase me to save face, then I must be disposable." This is how abandonment becomes inherited self-hatred. Not taught — absorbed. Not explained — felt.

And worse — we live in a culture that rewards this kind of betrayal. A mother who "holds her daughter accountable" is praised for her "tough love." A father who disowns a "wayward" son is seen as principled. Families that "distance themselves" from black sheep are seen as protecting their dignity. We confuse punishment with righteousness. We mistake moral cowardice for discipline. And the child pays the price — forever.

A child who is abandoned does not just question their parent. They question reality. "Is love real — or just conditional applause?" "Am I loved — or tolerated until I disappoint?" "Is my worth internal — or rented from others?" This is the hidden cost of moral disownment. It doesn't create moral clarity. It creates generational fracture. It doesn't purify the family. It poisons the child. And the worst part? Society claps.

Case Study: Cultural Revolution, China (1966–76)

When ideological purity eclipsed family, children turned on their own blood.

In Mao Zedong's China, teenagers were encouraged to expose their parents as "counter-revolutionaries."
Sons handed over fathers.
Daughters denounced mothers.
Parents were dragged into public squares, imprisoned, executed — all in the name of loyalty to the collective.

Love wasn't sacred.
The tribe was.

To prove their purity, children sacrificed their protectors.
Not because they were evil — but because the system taught them that obedience was virtue, and family was expendable.

That is the power of collective moral performance.
That is the cost when belonging demands blood.

Chapter 9

LOYALTY ENDS AT EXPOSURE

"We are friends — until the crowd is watching."

Friendship as Moral Camouflage

We like to think of friendship as sacred — a bond immune to the winds of circumstance. A place where masks fall away, where our ugliest truths are held without fear. But that's a fantasy. A lovely one. A comforting one. And like most comforting ideas — it collapses under pressure. Scratch beneath the surface of most adult friendships, and you will not find unwavering loyalty.

You will find **mutual image management** — an unspoken agreement to uphold each other's reputations so long as the arrangement remains convenient.
"I support you… as long as your shame doesn't splash onto me." "I believe in you… as long as the mob isn't watching." "I'll hold your secret… until it costs me nothing."
Friendship, for many, is not a commitment. It is **a contract**. And the fine print reads: *You are safe here — unless your downfall threatens my reflection.*
When your name becomes radioactive — when your face appears next to controversy, scandal, or accusation — you will not be punished by enemies. You will be erased by friends.
Not because they hate you. But because you have become **inconvenient**.

Psychological Reflex, Not Cruelty

We are tribal beings. Our brains evolved in villages where exile meant death. Social approval is not a luxury — it is a survival mechanism. When someone near us is cast out, our primitive circuitry lights up:
- *Distance yourself.*
- *Deny affiliation.*
- *Signal loyalty to the tribe, not the outcast.*

This is not modern cowardice. It is ancient wiring. And the more "modern" and "moral" a society pretends to be, the more it relies on **ritual disavowals** to maintain the illusion of integrity.

When Crisis Reveals Character

Real friendship does not reveal itself in joy, success, or celebration. It reveals itself in disgrace. In collapse. In accusation.

That's when the masks fall — not from the one exposed, but from those who once stood beside them.

Some will flee. Some will post something vague and safe. Some will ghost you, hoping the silence won't be noticed. Some will nod sympathetically while secretly adjusting their distance to protect their own image.

And a few — a rare few — will stay. Not because you are innocent. But because you are human.

And those are your friends. The rest were merely allies of convenience — strangers with mutual benefit.

The Industry of Abandonment

In the digital age, friendship is more performative than ever. We curate relationships like portfolios — adding and deleting based on optics. A single accusation, a misinterpreted post, a past mistake resurrected by the crowd — and a friend becomes a liability.

- Corporate friendships vanish in press releases.
- Academic friendships disappear behind institutional memos.
- Personal friendships dissolve in unread messages and cold silence.

We don't mourn the loss. We rewrite the memory: *"They changed."* Or worse: *"I never really knew them."*

This isn't honesty. It's self-protection disguised as reflection.

Case Study: Jonah Lehrer

Jonah Lehrer was a rising star — a bestselling author, Rhodes scholar, and science writer hailed as a public intellectual. Then, in 2012, it was revealed he had fabricated quotes and reused his own work across publications without citation.

In weeks, his speaking invitations evaporated. Colleagues who had praised his brilliance deleted tweets, disavowed collaborations, and issued statements of shock. Not one defended his humanity — only their own distance from the scandal.

Jonah Lehrer was not guilty of violence, exploitation, or hatred. He was guilty of imperfection in a field obsessed with the illusion of moral precision. And when his reputation cracked, the same media outlets that once built him now used him for clicks and cautionary tales.

The lesson: You are only safe while you are useful. When you stumble, the crowd doesn't ask if you can be redeemed — they ask *"Who's next?"*

Why Exposure Breaks the Bond

When someone close to you falls — not in battle, but in reputation — the ground doesn't just shift beneath *them*. It shifts beneath *you*. They get caught cheating. They go bankrupt. They're exposed for a lie, a failure, a secret they couldn't hold any longer. Maybe it's a careless tweet, a scandal in the press, or a whisper that went viral.

They are still the same person. But now they're radioactive.

And so you face a moral test — not about them, but about *you*: Do you stay near the fallout? Do you defend someone publicly disgraced? Or do you quietly step back — recalibrate, reframe, and protect your own standing?

Most people choose safety.

Not because they've stopped caring. But because proximity to shame is socially fatal. Exposure doesn't just break the fallen. It breaks those tethered to them — unless they cut the rope.

And so they do.

They say nothing.

The Sudden Silence

There is no confrontation. No screaming. No slammed doors. No betrayals with names. Just *absence*. A soft erasure.

The phone stops ringing. The WhatsApp group goes quiet. Your name disappears from invites, stories, feeds, and profiles. You are no longer discussed — you are simply gone.

Some justify their silence as neutrality: *"I'm staying out of it."* But neutrality in these moments is a costume. Beneath it is fear. And fear does what fear has always done: it isolates the infected.

What you feel isn't rejection. It's the disorientation of becoming invisible. The people who once toasted you now sip in silence. The friends who once swore loyalty now speak only in disclaimers. Your name, once linked to dinners, projects, laughter — now floats unspoken in rooms where you once belonged.

It is not betrayal in the traditional sense. It is passive abandonment. And it cuts deeper because it's done *without* cruelty. Just distance. Just stillness. It is exile dressed in quiet.

Social Death After Scandal

Imagine a man — ambitious, generous, social — caught up in a business scandal. He misrepresented a deal. It wasn't violent. It wasn't predatory. But it was public, embarrassing, and moral ambiguity isn't tolerated in a world built on optics.

In the first few hours, messages flood in: *"I'm so sorry, bro."* But by the second day, the tone shifts. By the third, the feed dries up.

• His WhatsApp thread — once daily chatter — hasn't buzzed in 72 hours.

• A dinner invitation is quietly retracted. *"Let's catch up another time."*

• *His mentor posts a vague tweet: "Accountability is everything — no exceptions."*

• Friends see him online but don't click. Don't check in. Don't ask.

He is not alone because he's a monster. He is alone because he became a liability. And in a moral economy driven by perception, loyalty costs too much.

The truth is brutal: most friendships are not unconditional. They are stable under praise. Fragile under shame. What breaks them is not disagreement — but **exposure**. And what holds them together isn't love — it's **mutual benefit**, dissolved the moment that benefit disappears.

The friend who leaves when you fall wasn't fake. They were *real*, within the terms you never realized existed.

Until the day you breached them.

The Social Brain is Wired for Survival, Not Loyalty

We like to imagine ourselves as loyal — steadfast, principled, the kind of people who stand by our friends when the wind changes. But that's fantasy. Biology tells another story.

The human brain — particularly the *social brain* — did not evolve for truth, or loyalty, or justice. It evolved for **survival**. In early tribal societies, your greatest threat wasn't a wild animal. It was being **excluded**.

To be cast out was to die slowly — from starvation, exposure, or predator attack. So we learned, generation after generation, to read the room. To adjust. To align. To distance ourselves from the tainted before the tribe looked our way.

If the chieftain turned against someone, it didn't matter what they did. You stepped back. Or you stepped into the fire with them.

We still do it today — only the language has changed.

- **HR calls it "protecting the brand."**
- Friends call it **"boundaries."**
- **Colleagues call it "letting things play out."**
- **Brands call it "pausing our relationship."**
- Media calls it **"distancing."**

But underneath it all, it's the same primal algorithm: **"They're burning. I don't want to smell like smoke."**

The Language of Abandonment

After a fall from grace, the chorus begins — soft, rehearsed, and eerily identical:

- *"We were close… once."*
- *"She wasn't the same lately."*
- *"I didn't really know him like that."*

These aren't necessarily lies. They're **survival statements** — a performance for the crowd to prove one's own moral insulation. They are the social equivalent of stepping away from a collapsing building and declaring, *"I never lived there."*

Because in the modern economy of reputation, the question isn't, *"Who do you love?"* It's *"Who are you seen loving when the mob is watching?"*

People don't often betray with swords. They betray with **shrugs**. With **invisible edits**. With the soft deletion of connection.

And it hurts not because they said something cruel — but because they said **nothing** at all.

No call. No message. No defense. Just absence. An eerie silence where loyalty used to be.

Evolutionary Reflex, Modern Disguise

We praise loyalty in speeches. We toast to it at weddings. But when the storm hits, **loyalty is the first thing thrown overboard.** Why? Because our nervous system doesn't want virtue. It wants safety.

This is **neurobiological triage** — The amygdala scanning not for truth or injustice, but for **risk proximity**.

And so the friend who once called you "family" Now avoids eye contact in the hallway. The colleague who vouched for your character now forwards HR your emails. The mentor who called you "brilliant" now tells others *"I always had doubts."*

It's not always malice. It's **tribal reflex** in a modern suit.

The Most Painful Betrayals Are Often the Quietest

You don't get stabbed in the back. You just get… **removed**. From the invite list. From the comments. From the conversation.

The people you defended won't defend you. The ones you celebrated won't remember your name. The ones you saved will tell others they barely knew you.

And that's the deepest wound: To be **unmade** by people who once swore they'd stand with you.

Not because they changed their mind — but because **you changed your status.**

And in a world addicted to moral optics, status contamination is unforgivable.

Why Silence Hurts More Than Condemnation

Condemnation wounds the ego. But **silence** wounds the soul.

When someone confronts you, you still exist to them. You are still a character in their moral universe — even if cast as the villain. But when they go silent? They don't just step away. They rewrite the script and remove you from the stage.

No defense. No farewell. Just absence — cold, clean, and deniable.

And in that vacuum, you begin to ask unanswerable questions: Was I ever really loved? Were we ever really close? Did I matter — or was I just a convenience until I made things inconvenient?

This is the brutal paradox of social collapse: It's not the mob that hurts most. It's the friend who won't look at you. The partner who disappears from the thread. The mentor who posts vaguely about "accountability." The loved one who says *"I'm staying out of it,"* when you needed them most.

Their silence is not neutral. It is a **calculation**.

A strategic distancing — made not from principle, but self-preservation. **Because in a world governed by image, the unspoken creed is clear: "I will not bleed with you. I will not burn with you. I will not be seen next to your wreckage."**

And in that moment, silence becomes complicity. Not just in your public fall — But in the private death of the bond you thought was real.

The Existential Violence of Disappearance

What makes this kind of betrayal so devastating isn't just the abandonment. It's the **erasure**.

Your story — everything shared, earned, endured together — is quietly deleted from their narrative. You are no longer mentioned. No longer defended. No longer remembered.

They walk back through the timeline and retroactively decide: *You never really mattered.*

This isn't disagreement. It's exile.

It's being turned into a ghost while still breathing.

And the cruelest part? They still consider themselves good. They still sleep at night. Because they didn't attack you. They didn't defame you. They just said nothing.

But in a moral crisis, **silence is not absence of action.** It is action.

It says to the mob: "I'm not one of them."

It says to the crowd: "Don't worry — I'll help you look away."

Love That Disappears Was Never Love

If your fall from grace makes someone flee, They were never standing with you — only near you. And if your disgrace makes someone forget who you are, then who they were beside you was also a performance.

This is the truth we try not to see: **Most relationships are not built on love.** They are built on **mutual safety**.

But the test of love — real love — is not how people stand by you in glory. It's how they **stand with you in collapse**.

And by that measure, most people fail. Not because they are evil. But because **they are scared.**

Because the deepest human instinct is not to protect others — It is to survive the crowd.

And so they disappear. And their silence becomes the final betrayal — Not of your actions… But of your shared past, Your unspoken bond, Your belief that they would stay.

And once that silence takes root — It echoes louder than any scream.

Chapter 10

THE DEATH OF THE INNER LIFE

"When the world becomes your audience, the soul has nowhere to grow."

The Vanishing Interior

There was a time when life unfolded inwardly. Thoughts were private terrain. Feelings were not content. Regret, doubt, conviction — these were wrestled with in solitude, not outsourced to comment sections. There was a time when morality was something you lived with, not something you performed. Who you were was shaped in silence — in the quiet ache of your own conscience, in the long hours of reckoning no one saw.

But now, if it isn't posted, it didn't happen. If it isn't praised, it isn't good. If it isn't visible, it isn't real.

We live in a world where everything must be witnessed to exist — and *approved* to survive. The self has become an exhibition. Privacy has become suspicion. And the interior life — that sacred space where nuance lives, where contradictions are held without resolution, where the soul whispers in a voice only you can hear — is being erased.

We no longer pause. We post. We no longer wrestle. We react. Every thought is interrupted by its imagined audience. Every feeling is filtered through potential backlash. We ask not "Is this right?" but "Will this be liked?" The conscience doesn't disappear. It is replaced — by the algorithm.

We curate ourselves with surgical precision, building identities that will pass moral inspection but cannot survive silence. Complexity is punished. Ambiguity is unsafe. So we amputate the parts of ourselves that might offend, and we grow new ones shaped by reward.

This is not self-awareness. It's self-erasure.
This is not evolution. It's evacuation.
Of the soul. Of the mind. Of the very possibility of becoming real.

We scroll through endless avatars performing goodness, grief, passion, justice — and yet behind the glass, there is nothing solid. No root system. No interior scaffolding. Just performance, metrics, and the creeping terror of being unseen. The audience is always watching. So we are always acting. And in the theatre of modern morality, the first thing to die is truth. But what follows, quietly and without protest, is something even more fragile.

The inner life.
The only place left where real character could have survived.

The Mirror That Never Breaks

The mirror no longer breaks — because it is made of code, not glass. It reflects endlessly, without distortion, without escape. And in that reflection, we are slowly disappearing.

Social media was sold as a window to the world — a portal to connection, dialogue, discovery. But it mutated. It became a mirror with no back. Every action, every thought, every piece of self must be displayed. Measured. Rated. Perceived.

We no longer ask, What do I believe?
We ask:
How will this look?
What will they think?
Will this be misunderstood?
Will this cost me?

The moment a thought is born, it is scanned for compliance. The moment a feeling stirs, it is screened for risk. We begin editing before we've even begun feeling. We rehearse every word. We rehearse how to appear unrehearsed. And in doing so, we carve away our private self in tiny, daily amputations.

This is not expression. It's erosion.

The self becomes not a soul — but a feed.
Not a person — but a performance reel.
Not a journey — but a product line.

You are no longer allowed to think in silence, to doubt in peace, to wrestle without witness. Even your confessions must be branded. Even your grief must be shareable.

You're not punished for being wrong.
You're punished for being unfiltered.

And so, we construct a version of ourselves optimized for applause.
We sharpen it with hashtags.
We polish it with filters.
We update it with trends.
We delete the parts that don't perform.

But here's the tragedy: the mirror reflects, but it never sees. It cannot understand you. It cannot love you. It cannot forgive you.

It is permanent exposure with no intimacy.
Permanent connection with no understanding.
Permanent judgment with no redemption.

And yet we stare into it. We feed it. We dance for it. We lose sleep over it.
Why?
Because the mirror offers something more addictive than truth — *approval*.

So we become what they clap for.
What they'll retweet.
What they'll hire.
What they'll not cancel.

Until the soul itself becomes foreign — a voice you hear only faintly, and only when the battery dies.

Why Virtue Can't Survive Constant Exposure

Virtue is not a show.
It is not scalable.
It does not perform well under lights.

True virtue is agonizingly private — formed in the dark furnace of difficult choices, unseen sacrifices, and inner wars no one claps for.
But today, nothing is real unless it's seen.
And nothing is good unless it is celebrated.

This is the sickness: **we've mistaken validation for verification**.
We think a flood of approval makes something more moral.
We think applause is evidence of integrity.
But in truth, **every time virtue is dragged into the spotlight, it starts to rot.**

Because exposure demands simplification.
Performance demands clarity.
And real virtue is neither.

It is messy. Self-doubting. Uncomfortable.
It often looks wrong before it proves right.
It sometimes offends before it heals.
It requires courage that has no audience, no reward, no fanfare.

But the internet cannot wait.
The feed must move.
So we strip virtue of its discomfort and package it for display.

We turn it into **branding**.
We attach hashtags.
We dress it in causes that will trend.
We sharpen its edges until no one bleeds and no one thinks.

And what remains is not virtue — but *the costume of virtue*.
Pre-digested. Palatable. Predictable.
The kind that will get you sponsored.
The kind that will get you hired.
The kind that will keep the mob from tearing you apart.

But here's the horror:
The more you perform goodness, the less capable you become of actually doing it.

Why?

Because you stop building the muscles of moral resistance.
You stop listening to the inner voice.
You forget how to stand alone.

You begin editing your values in real-time, reshaping your ethics mid-sentence, censoring your gut in anticipation of what the crowd will find "appropriate."
And once you do that long enough — **you no longer have a moral spine.**

You only have *settings*.
You only have *modes*.
You only have *adaptive behavior* — like a hunted animal learning not to bleed where predators gather.

This is not virtue.
This is **neurological compliance**.

You are not good.
You are *trained*.

When Conscience Becomes Crowd-Sourced

Once, conscience was a private war.
Now, it's a group chat.

The voice that once whispered from deep within — flawed, trembling, sacred — has been drowned out by the roar of comment sections, polls, DMs, and dopamine-triggered conformity.
We don't ask ourselves what's right anymore.
We ask: *What's trending?*

We have outsourced our moral compass to the crowd — a crowd that is blind, angry, addicted, and constantly hungry for someone to burn.

This is the new morality: don't ask what's true. Ask what won't get you killed.

We've mistaken the algorithm for the oracle.
Mistaken virality for virtue.
Mistaken retweets for righteousness.

But here is the horror underneath:

> The human brain was not built for this.
> Your conscience — the fragile internal regulator of guilt, shame, pride, and fear — was never designed to be networked across ten thousand strangers watching your every move.

It cannot survive it.
It doesn't evolve. It deforms.

Neuroscience confirms it: the more eyes watching you, the more your brain flips from **reflection** to **reaction**.
Moral reasoning shuts down.
Fight-or-flight kicks in.
You are no longer choosing between right and wrong — you're choosing between *execution* and *escape*.

And so we adapt.

We shape our ethics not around truth, but **around terror**.
We study the terrain like prisoners watching guards.
We mimic the slogans. We echo the outrage. We learn to pass the purity tests — not because we believe, but because we fear.

This is not conscience.
It is behavioral conditioning through mass surveillance.

You twitch when you're supposed to twitch.
You bark when you're supposed to bark.
You flinch when the tone shifts — even if you don't know why.

And the worst part? You think it's you.
You think you're growing. You think you're becoming "better."
But you're not. You're **being trained like an animal in a cage with invisible bars made of social feedback loops.**

You are punished not for being immoral —
but for being *off-script*.
And rewarded not for being good —
but for being **predictable**.

So conscience dies.

Not with a scream, not with a collapse —
but with a **slow substitution**.
Its voice replaced by likes.
Its pain replaced by anxiety.
Its solitude replaced by panic that you're no longer in sync with the tribe.

And what fills the void where conscience used to live?

A hollow algorithm that punishes ambiguity.
A moral hivemind that flattens thought into echo.
An audience that demands your soul, pixel by pixel — then scrolls on without remembering your name.

Privacy Was Never About Secrecy — It Was About Sanctity

We were told that privacy was for the guilty.
That if you had nothing to hide, you had nothing to fear.
But that was a lie.
A devastating, civilization-eroding lie.

Because privacy was never about hiding.
It was about **becoming**.

A private life is where identity is born in its rawest, bloodiest, most unmarketable form.
It is the sanctuary where truth can be ugly without consequence.
Where doubt can stretch its legs without punishment.
Where belief can stutter and change without needing to make a public apology.

Privacy is not concealment.
It is incubation.

A soul cannot form under constant scrutiny.
Character cannot develop in front of a crowd.
Transformation requires silence, slowness, and room for contradiction — all of which are annihilated by the **performance culture of permanent exposure**.

We don't grow under observation.
We *adjust*.

We twitch, edit, reframe, delete.
We are no longer discovering who we are — we are **testing which version of ourselves gets the best engagement.**

And so, in the absence of privacy, the self fractures.

You become many versions of yourself, split across platforms, contexts, tones, and audiences.
A thousand masks. A thousand fragments.
All tailored to be tolerable. All filtered to be safe.

But here's the truth no one wants to hear:

> **If you cannot exist unobserved, you do not exist at all.**

If you cannot think without fear, your mind is not free.
If you cannot feel without feedback, your emotions are not real.
If you cannot wrestle without witnesses, you have no conscience — only compliance.

What dies when privacy dies is not reputation.
It is **soul depth**.
Moral depth.
The ability to be a full human being instead of a curated persona.

This is the final horror:

We didn't lose privacy.
We *gave it away*.
We bartered it for attention.
We traded it for speed.
We sacrificed it to avoid the terror of being alone with ourselves.

Because that is what modern life fears more than cancellation, more than failure, more than death itself —

To be alone.
With the unedited self.
With the unfiltered mind.
With the naked truth of who we are when no one is watching.

And yet, that was the only place where redemption could begin.

Not in the light.
Not in the feed.
But in the **quiet furnace of privacy** —
Where the self, trembling and unliked, might finally be real.

The Spiritual Cost of Always Being Seen

To be human is to wrestle.
To sit in the dark with thoughts too complex for language.
To feel without narrating.
To sin, to ache, to doubt — and to emerge changed, not exposed.

But in an age of permanent visibility, this human process is collapsing.
There is no room to unravel. No space to contradict yourself.
You are always watched —
By followers.
By bosses.
By family.
By the ambient surveillance of the digital collective.

And so, you begin to amputate.

You suppress the parts of yourself that don't serve the performance.
You kill your edges, your oddities, your shadows — anything that might threaten the illusion.
And over time, the self becomes:

- Cautious
- Sanitized
- Predictable
- Spiritually emaciated

This is not growth.
This is **moral anorexia** — starving the soul for the approval of strangers.
This is not self-control.
This is **slow spiritual suicide**, disguised as discipline.

We no longer become who we are in solitude.
We become who we are under observation.

Every moment is filtered through a lens of potential judgment.
Every thought is interrogated by the imaginary tribunal of "they."

> **You are what they see.**
> **You are what they measure.**
> **You are what they reward.**

And your brain rewires itself to comply.

Neuroscientists have a name for this: **neuroplastic adaptation under social stress.**
You begin to *feel differently* because you anticipate how others will perceive those feelings.
You start to think in metrics.
To filter emotion before it arrives.
To package your interior world into something digestible, likeable, postable.

You become a **brand manager of the soul**.
Your joy must be photogenic.
Your grief must be narratable.
Your virtue must be hashtagged.
Even your outrage must hit the right tone — or you're punished.

This is not transparency.
It is **emotional taxidermy** — preserving expressions of humanity in curated poses, emptied of life.

And it is exhausting.

We no longer reflect — we scroll.
We don't rest — we decompress.
We don't confess — we perform remorse.
Even our apologies are trialed for optics before spoken.

In this theater of perpetual exposure, we are always:
- Editing
- Softening
- Diluting
- Rehearsing
- Smiling through the exhaustion of self-maintenance

We are not being ourselves.
We are being versions of ourselves that won't be punished.

And so, a silent atrocity takes place:
We become strangers to our own interiors.
We feel only echoes.
We touch emotions faintly — too busy scanning for risk to actually *feel* anything real.

Because the soul cannot deepen when the self is constantly being rehearsed.

Because no one can become whole
in a room that never turns off the lights.

The Death of Solitude

Real solitude is more than being alone.
It is **being unwatched**, undistracted, undivided.
It is the last remaining chamber of the soul,
where there is no audience, no interface, no echo.
Only you —
and what you've buried.

And in that confrontation comes pain.
But also truth.
Because solitude is where you meet your contradictions.

Your cowardice.
Your secret cruelties.
Your primal instincts clawing beneath the surface of your performance.

> It is the silence that strips away the costume and says: *Now show me who you really are.*

And from that terror — slowly, with no witness and no applause — comes the possibility of moral growth.

But that possibility is disappearing.
Because solitude is becoming extinct.

We are never alone.
We are plugged in. Pacified. Occupied.

We listen to podcasts in the shower.
We answer emails on the toilet.
We "meditate" with apps that track our serenity like a heart rate monitor.
Even silence has been colonized.
Even introspection has been monetized.

We don't sit with our minds.
We outsource them.

And so even spirituality — once the final refuge of the inner life — has been dragged into the marketplace of mirrors.
- Meditation is now gamified.
- Prayer is posted.
- Gratitude is branded.
- Stillness is sold back to us as a productivity hack.

We no longer seek transcendence.
We consume it.

We don't do inner work.
We **perform** the aesthetic of inner work.
Mindfulness becomes marketing.
Healing becomes content.
Spirituality becomes a status signal wrapped in robes and hashtags.

We tell ourselves we're awakening — but we're just applying a brighter filter to the same cracked mirror.

And here is the consequence no one speaks of:

> When you lose the ability to be alone,
> **you lose the ability to be moral.**

Because all great moral traditions —
whether carved in scripture or inked in philosophy —
rest on the same sacred assumption:
That some truths only arrive when the noise dies.

When the feed stops.
When the mirrors are covered.
When the self is stripped of audience.

Without solitude, there is no self.
Without a self, there is no conscience.
Without conscience, morality becomes mimicry — tribal, reactive, preloaded.

And that, perhaps, is the plan.

Because tribal coherence thrives best when the individual goes missing.
When solitude dies, programming begins.
You become fully editable.
A shell, ready to be filled by the feed.

You don't resist the crowd — because you no longer know where the crowd ends and *you* begin.

Eulogy for the Soul

The death of the inner life is not loud.
It doesn't make headlines.
There is no siren, no collapse, no final gasp.

It dies **quietly**.
In a million flickers of the screen.
In a thousand tiny compromises.
In the slow erosion of privacy, of solitude, of space to think without consequence.

It dies when you check how your face looks while crying.
When you adjust a confession for tone.
When you feel an emotion and immediately wonder how it might be captioned.

The soul is not killed.
It is **crowded out**.

By notifications.
By judgment.
By the relentless pressure to be seen, and approved, and applauded — even in your darkest hours.

> And one day, without ceremony or warning,
> you wake up as someone who is always speaking, always broadcasting, always adjusting —
> but who no longer knows what you truly believe.

Because the voice inside — the one that once whispered, challenged, wrestled —
has grown so faint beneath the algorithms and applause,
that you start to think it was never real to begin with.

The soul doesn't scream when it dies.
It just **stops speaking**.
And we call the silence "maturity."
We call the numbness "resilience."
We call the performance "identity."

But make no mistake:

> This is not growth.
> It is *evacuation*.
> Not evolution — but extinction.
> Of solitude. Of depth. Of the only thing that ever made you real.

And in the end, we don't become better.
We become *manageable*.
We don't become more loving.
We become **more compatible with the feed**.
More reactive. More signal-ready. Less human.

This is the eulogy no one reads:

> *Here lies the inner life.*
> *Once sacred. Now streamlined.*
> *Once private. Now monetized.*
> *Once a soul. Now a brand.*

❖❖❖

Chapter 11

RIGHTEOUSNESS IS A COSTUME

"We don't seek to be good. We seek to look good — in the language of our tribe."

The Costume of Conscience

Righteousness was once a battle.

A bruising, soul-wrenching confrontation with one's own darkness.
It demanded introspection, contradiction, humility.
It came slowly — if ever — after pain, doubt, failure, and the long loneliness of moral reckoning.

But that kind of righteousness doesn't sell.
It doesn't trend.
It's hard to photograph.

So we replaced it.

We stripped virtue of its weight and replaced it with **wardrobe**.

Now we **wear** our conscience.
- Correct terminology
- Social justice slogans
- Political badges
- Health-conscious habits
- Curated, crowd-safe opinions

This is not about belief.
It's about *alignment* — with the moral aesthetic of the moment.
It's about showing that you belong to the righteous tribe, that your conscience has been pre-approved, pre-assembled, and is ready for public use.

You no longer have to be a good person.
You just have to dress like one.

The conscience becomes costume.
Not because people are evil —
but because we've made real moral struggle **intolerable**.

There's no time for nuance.
No patience for slow convictions.
No tolerance for complexity.
So instead of doing the hard internal work of transformation, we costume ourselves in *moral branding*.

We signal fluency in the latest cause.
We swap belief for compliance.
We replace private wrestling with public recitation.

And we tell ourselves we're growing.
But really, we're **styling our morality like an outfit**,
changing it depending on who's watching,
what's safe to say,
and what will get us liked — or at least not attacked.

This is not evolution.
This is **camouflage**.
This is the hunted learning how to blend in with the moral terrain to avoid being devoured.

But here's the tragedy:

>A costume can protect you.
>But it can never *save* you.

Because when conscience is reduced to costume,
when righteousness becomes a skin you wear instead of a soul you build

you lose the ability to change.

Not in public.
Not in real time.
Not with the crowd watching.

You just get better at pretending.
More fluent in the right scripts.
More skilled at hiding your real thoughts under the gloss of moral fashion.

And somewhere inside,
the part of you that *could* have grown —
the part of you that *wanted* to be better —
starves in silence, waiting for the lights to go off.

From Virtue to Branding

Character used to be carved out of crisis.
It was forged in silence, failure, and the unbearable intimacy of confronting who you actually are.
It took years.
It left scars.

You couldn't borrow it.
You couldn't fake it.
And most of the time, no one even saw it.

But in today's moral economy, character is obsolete.
It takes too long.
It doesn't scale.
It doesn't generate engagement.

So we replaced it with something faster.
More visual.
More responsive to public pressure.

We replaced it with **branding**.

You don't need to live well anymore.
You just need to **look aligned**.

Modern morality is now a press kit —
A curated feed of symbols that signal you are on the "right side."
- Post the quote.
- Condemn the right villain.
- Add the flag.
- Use the hashtag.
- Echo the language of the moment with surgical precision.

We think we're building moral credibility.
But we're actually building *personal brands with ethical logos* —
Visibly righteous, algorithmically safe, spiritually hollow.

What was once an identity shaped by conscience is now just:
- A profile
- A pose
- A tagline
- A PR strategy for not getting exiled from the digital village

And here's the chilling reality:

> You no longer need to *be good*.
> You just need to appear morally up-to-date.

We're not wrestling with right and wrong.
We're studying trends.

We're scanning for what will get us hired, liked, retweeted, or — at minimum — *not destroyed*.

We don't build values anymore.
We **subscribe to them**, like updates — and when the culture changes, so do we.
Not because we've grown.
But because we're trying to avoid being on the wrong side of history — not by doing good,
but by **looking compatible** with whoever writes the next version of the story.

And in the process, we lose the one thing real virtue requires:
The courage to stand *alone* in your truth —
before it's popular,
before it's safe,
before it's been branded.

The Corporate Costume of Humility

In the professional theatre of LinkedIn, **humility has become a costume** — carefully stitched from phrases that appear self-effacing but are loaded with **strategic ego**.

We've all seen the script:
"I'm humbled to have been recognised by [X]." "Feeling honoured to be invited to speak at [Y]." "Truly grateful to be selected for [Z]…"

On the surface, these sound like modest reflections. But read them again — slowly. These are not expressions of humility. They are **coded announcements of superiority**, disguised as virtue.
To say *"I'm humbled to be chosen"* is not humility. It's status signaling dressed in modesty drag.

This isn't an attack on achievement — it's a critique of the **dishonest framing** of self-promotion as moral virtue. These posts don't just say *"Look what I've done."* They say: *"Look what I've done — and how spiritually pure I am while doing it."*

More Examples of Performative Humility in Corporate Disguise:

• *"I never expected this recognition, but I'm honoured to receive it."* → *Translation: I absolutely expected it. And you should know I got it.*
• *"I'm incredibly grateful to join this brilliant team of leaders."* → *Translation: I've entered a new tier of power. Applaud me accordingly.*
• *"I'm not usually one to post, but this means a lot…"* → *Translation: I post when the attention ROI is high enough.*
• *"Truly blessed to have been included in this year's Top 100 Innovators."* → *Translation: Yes, I'm elite. But see? I'm also humble and spiritual.*

This isn't humility. It's public relations for the ego.
It's what happens when **social media collapses identity and performance** into a single act of branding. You're no longer just a professional. You're now expected to be a **professionally curated moral person** — always grateful, always honoured, always gracious — even as you **self-advertise with surgical precision.**

Why This Matters:

In a culture where **visibility is virtue**, the mask of humility **insulates ego from critique**. You can't question someone who's "just grateful." You can't critique someone who's "honoured." You can't challenge someone who "wasn't even expecting it."
So the post becomes **bulletproof moral camouflage** — not because it's sincere, but because it's emotionally unassailable.
This is not the death of humility — It's humility weaponized as a form of personal branding.

And the worst part?
We all know it. We scroll. We wince. We see the performance — and many perform right back.
Because this is how status is now exchanged: Through **ritualized declarations of virtue**, wrapped in soft words, delivered at scale.

The Echo Chamber of Ritual Praise

But the post is only half the theatre.
What completes the performance is the **ritual praise parade** that follows in the comments — a carefully coded chorus of applause disguised as camaraderie:

"So proud of you, legend." "Such an honour to have worked with you on this." "Well deserved — you're truly an inspiration." "Absolutely no one better for this than you." "Congrats on such an amazing achievement!"

These replies are rarely about the achievement. They're about **being seen clapping**.
Because in these social ecosystems, **not clapping makes you suspicious**. Praise becomes **a loyalty ritual** — and the cost of not participating is exclusion.
It's moral performance **mirrored back and forth**, in a loop of simulated sincerity:
• The poster feigns humility.
• The audience feigns admiration.
• Everyone maintains the illusion that **something virtuous just happened.**
But nothing virtuous happened. No wisdom was shared. No truth was risked. No honesty was expressed. Just another round of **emotional laundering**, where ego goes in and "gratitude" comes out — with the community there to validate the process like polite moral accountants.

And if you don't join in? You're *cold*. You're *bitter*. You *don't support others*.

Because this isn't just performance. It's **tribal obedience, algorithmically rewarded.**

The Morality of Mimicry

In a world where virtue is a spectacle, true moral action has been replaced by an art of imitation.
We no longer labor to understand or transform; we simply mimic the appearance of goodness.

You don't have to study the cause.
You don't have to do the hard work.
All you need is to repost the trending narrative.

- **Understand the cause?**
  Just hit "share."
  The details, the nuance, the sacrifice — they're all collateral to a swipe.
- **Do the hard work?**
  Instead, give praise where it's convenient.
  Signal applause, applaud from the sidelines, and let someone else shoulder the grind.
- **Take a stand?**
  Simply signal your membership in the "right side."
  A hashtag, a retweet, a status update — these are your battle scars in a moral war that no longer requires real commitment.

This mimicry is more than shallow performance; it's a kind of **social camouflage.**
It's the reflex to kneel immediately, to join the chorus of applause without ever really questioning the tune.

In this age, you are evaluated not by the truths you build or the struggles you endure, but by how quickly you align with the trending indignation.

Your moral value is measured in microseconds — in the speed of your capitulation.

And so, we all learn the lesson:

> The measure of your integrity is not what you stand for, but how swiftly you kneel.

Moral mimicry offers a seductive ease.
It's risk-free and always on sale.
By blending in with the tribe's ever-shifting moral colors, you avoid the scrutiny of depth, the discomfort of introspection, the rigors of authentic choice.

This is not a commitment to goodness — it is a transaction in solidarity, a superficial marking of territory in a digital coliseum.
It's the idea that you don't have to build character or understand suffering; you just have to simulate the behavior of the "good."

And while you perform, the genuine article, the raw, unfiltered self that once contended with life's brutal truths, slowly evaporates—
Dissolving under the pressure of being nothing more than a mirror reflecting a pre-approved facade.

In this counterfeit morality, real conscience is sacrificed at the altar of convenience.
The quickness to kneel has become the new currency.
And in a market where authenticity is the first casualty, you can no longer tell if the act of doing good is a brave stand or just another well-rehearsed move in a dance of pretense.

Corporate Wokeness and the Moral Shell Game

Modern morality is no longer measured in actions — but aesthetics.

Consider the new case study in performative virtue: the modern corporation.

These are entities that:
- Exploit labor in invisible supply chains
- Wreck ecosystems under the guise of "efficiency"
- Funnel billions through tax loopholes while communities starve

And yet — without irony, without shame — they will:
- Post black squares on Instagram
- Rebrand logos with rainbow filters every June
- **Pledge carbon neutrality by 2050 while emitting record CO_2 today**

This isn't transformation.
It's **costume design**.

The outfit is ethical.
The applause is automated.
The soul is absent.

> It is righteousness as a *cover story* —
> a carefully stitched mask of conscience worn by entities **incapable of guilt.**

Corporations aren't repenting.
They're adapting.
They are learning the choreography of performative goodness —
because in the morality economy, looking aligned is more profitable than being accountable.

And here's the dark truth:
It works.

Why?

Because we — the audience — no longer want depth.
We want **signals**.

We are a culture:
- Overstimulated by spectacle
- Addicted to speed
- Suspicious of nuance
- Uncomfortable with anything not publicly declared

We do not have time for moral complexity.
We want clarity at a glance.
Virtue must now come pre-labeled, pre-approved, pre-shared.

> Why wrestle with truth when you can wear the correct uniform?
> Why risk discomfort when mimicry earns instant belonging?

And so we all — from corporations to individuals — begin to trade **integrity for insulation**.
Not goodness — but **safe positioning**.
Not moral courage — but **optical compliance**.

This isn't just a corporate trend.
It's a cultural collapse into performative safety.

We no longer ask if something is right.
We ask if it will offend the feed.
We no longer aspire to moral clarity.
We crave **moral camouflage.**

And while we're all staring at our reflections —
tweaking, adjusting, optimizing for applause —
we wonder why it all feels so hollow.

The answer is simple:

> The mirror doesn't judge.
> But it also doesn't care.

It reflects your moral costume, but never your conscience.
It flatters your performance, but never questions your foundation.
And you can spend your whole life inside it —
posing as righteous, while your soul slowly starves behind the glass.

Because a costume cannot transform you.

It can protect.
It can hide.
It can seduce the crowd.

But it cannot forge a self.

Real righteousness cannot be worn.
It cannot be bought.
It cannot be automated by PR.

It must be **suffered through**.
It must be **rebuilt from failure**.
It must be **earned in silence**, when no one is watching and no one will clap.

But that takes time.
And in the age of performance —
time is too expensive.

The Convenience of Performance

We were not taught to become good.
We were taught to become **unpunishable**.

To survive, we learned the choreography of moral optics —
how to pose just right,
how to echo the approved beliefs,
how to vanish anything that might be misread, misquoted, misunderstood.

> In a world where righteousness is a costume:
> - Truth becomes dangerous
> - Integrity becomes impractical
> - And the soul becomes secondary to optics

We don't fear being wrong anymore.
We fear being *seen without the right costume*.

So we assemble ourselves from fragments of moral aesthetics:

- The right hashtags
- The fashionable outrage
- The correct political alliances
- The sacred, photogenic causes

We parade these like badges.
We decorate our identity with them.
And then we stand very still, waiting for applause.

We tell ourselves this is virtue.
But deep down, **we know**:
We've abandoned the hard, bloody work of actual goodness for the glittering convenience of *looking good enough*.

This isn't just shallow.
It's pathological.

Because at the core of costume righteousness lies something darker:
Moral narcissism.

This isn't vanity of beauty — it's vanity of **virtue**.
It's not the need to *be* good —
It's the need to be **seen as good,** praised as good, and *never doubted* as good.

It is the hunger:
- To be viewed as "woke"
- To be applauded as "compassionate"
- To be loved for being on the "right side of history" — even if you've never lifted a finger to change it

Like all narcissism, moral narcissism is:
- Addicted to external validation
- Allergic to contradiction
- Incapable of self-reflection
- Trained to react with outrage, not introspection, when image is threatened

And so, modern righteousness becomes a mirror game.

The narcissist isn't obsessed with truth.
They're obsessed with their reflection in the eyes of others.

And now, so are we.

We don't ask: Am I just?
We ask: Do I appear just enough to survive this moment in public?

This is why:
- We have "activists" who organize nothing — but post endlessly.
- We have "allies" who collapse when you disagree with them.
- We have "leaders" who require applause to maintain composure.

Their goodness only exists as long as their image is fed.
Their conscience is tethered to the crowd.
Their moral compass spins toward whoever's watching.

And here is the final, devastating truth:

> Remove the mirror — and nothing remains.

No anchor.
No self.
No conviction.
Just the sound of performance with no audience to clap — and a soul that was never allowed to grow beneath the costume.

Narcissism Masquerading as Altruism

One of the darkest tricks of the ego is its ability to **masquerade self-service as self-sacrifice.**
The narcissist doesn't just seek admiration — they seek it dressed in the robes of virtue.
They want to be seen as **good**, not by being good, but by appearing to *suffer* for goodness.

And in our age, this camouflage is everywhere.

- Posts that "raise awareness" but always center the self
- Apologies that are choreographed not for repentance, but for redemption
- Public stances not taken to confront injustice, but to *earn virtue points*

"Look at how much I care."
"Look at how brave I am for speaking out."
"Look at how I supported the cause."

These are not sins of excess.
They are **sins of substitution** —
replacing private moral struggle with *public performance*.

The narcissist turns morality into a stage.
And the modern conscience has followed.

Why?

Because true virtue is hard.
It lives in ambiguity.
It suffers in silence.
It demands failure, repentance, contradiction, and the terrifying possibility of being wrong.

But the narcissistic moral performer — the one today's culture rewards — cannot tolerate that.

- They need **certainty**, not complexity
- They need **sides**, not spectrum
- They need **heroes and villains** — because nuance threatens the narrative
- And above all, they must always cast *themselves* as the hero

So they flatten the world.

- You're either righteous or evil.
- You're either with us or against us.
- There is no room for evolution — only allegiance.
- No space for contrition — only cancellation.

Because **contradiction threatens the image** —
and for the narcissist, the image *is* the self.
If the image dies, they do too.

And so we enter the final form of performance:

Righteousness as narcissistic theater.

A world of followers.
A world of mirrors.
A world where the soul is replaced by a script — and the audience decides your value.

We are seduced into:
- Caring more about applause than action
- Mistaking display for solidarity
- Confusing visibility with virtue
- Rehearsing empathy without ever feeling it

And like all narcissism, this ends not in glory, but in **collapse**.

Because when righteousness becomes a costume,
when goodness is merely a prop in the play of image maintenance —
the moment the applause stops,
the actor disappears too.

And underneath the polished performances is something terrifying:

A population that's highly visible… and internally lost.

We post more.
We perform more.
We signal more.

But we feel less.

Psychological studies confirm it:
Heavy social media users suffer lower self-esteem, deeper depression, and a disconnection from their own inner state.
They become skilled at expressing emotion *on cue* — but unable to distinguish whether they even feel it.

We are breeding a generation of moral performers who can perfectly articulate compassion, justice, identity —
while privately drowning in alienation, anxiety, and emotional disassociation.

They know the script.
They know the aesthetic.
They know how to survive the feed.

But what they don't know —
what we are now forgetting —
is how to sit in silence, wrestle with guilt, admit contradiction,
and slowly, painfully, become *someone real*.

Because when your morality is shaped by mirrors,
you learn to **pose**, not to grow.
And when the mirror breaks —
so do you.

Aftershock: The Silence Beneath the Applause

And so we stand —
polished, applauded, connected, *empty*.

We've mastered the art of looking righteous,
but forgotten the ache of becoming it.
We speak endlessly, but say nothing that costs us.
We confess publicly, but change nothing privately.
We wear virtue like armour —
not to protect what's sacred,
but to hide that we've hollowed out what once lived underneath.

And in our most honest, most private moments —
when the crowd is gone,
the phone is dark,

and no one is watching —
we feel it.

> The echo.
> The ache.
> The terrifying suspicion that we have become strangers to our own conscience.
> That somewhere along the line,
> we traded who we are for what they'd clap for.

And now we cannot find our way back.

Chapter 12

THE DISAPPEARING SELF

"The more I tried to belong, the less of me remained."

The Fragmented Identity

Modern life doesn't ask us to be whole.
It asks us to be **compatible**.

To belong, you must fracture.
To survive, you must edit.
To be accepted, you must perform a thousand versions of yourself — each calibrated to avoid rejection, each stripped of its inconvenient truths.

You must be:

- Confident, but self-effacing
- Political, but never polarizing
- Ambitious, but cloaked in humility
- Honest, but only in pre-approved doses
- Visible, but softened to avoid discomfort

So we begin to split.
We trim language.
We sand down opinions.
We rewrite our stories for different rooms.
We adjust tone based on what we sense will be tolerated.
We reshape allegiances not based on belief, but on *what won't get us burned*.

And slowly, almost imperceptibly, something terrifying happens:

> The original self — the one with contradiction, with fire, with sacred doubt — begins to disappear.

Not because it was wrong.
But because it was **inconvenient**.

And what takes its place is not a person.
It is a **persona** — a patchwork of traits optimized for applause, safety, and strategic alignment.

You don't speak your truth.
You *calculate* it.

You don't ask what you believe.
You *ask what won't cost you*.

You don't show up as a human being.
You *deploy* an identity.

It is soul fragmentation at scale —
the slow erosion of inner coherence under the acid rain of public performance.

And here is the brutal paradox:

> The more people you please, the less of you exists.

Because every adjustment, every silence, every performance made for belonging —
comes at the cost of some piece of your actual self.

You start to **disappear** in small, daily disappearances:
- The joke you don't tell
- The opinion you water down
- The grief you mute
- The belief you postpone
- The truth you erase to keep the peace

These aren't compromises.
They are **identity amputations**.

And over time, you don't even notice the bleeding.

Because the world keeps clapping.
Because the algorithm keeps rewarding.
Because the tribe keeps nodding.

But one day, in a rare moment of solitude,
you try to locate yourself —
the real self —
and there's nothing left to hold.

Only roles.
Only echoes.
Only the memory of a person you used to be before you edited them to death.

And this is the final tragedy:

> You win the acceptance of the world…
> and lose the ability to recognize your own reflection.

You've become *everybody's version of good* —
except your own.

You've been so many things to so many people
that you no longer remember who you were when you were no one's projection.

The self hasn't just been hidden.
It's been **replaced**.

And what remains is a mask that doesn't come off.
Even in the dark.
Even when no one is watching.
Because you no longer know what's underneath it.

The disappearance of the self isn't just a personal tragedy.
It's a relational one.
Because when you lose your interior, you don't just lose *you* —
you lose the ability to **connect**.

True connection requires **truth** —
but how can you offer truth when you no longer know what yours is?

You smile.
You nod.
You say the right things.
But deep down, you know:

> No one is loving *you*.
> They're loving the character you cast for them.

And so, even in intimacy, you feel alone.
Even when surrounded, you feel unknown.
You can't receive love because part of you knows it's not you being loved —

it's your **compliance.**

Your friendships become performances.
Your partnerships become brand alignments.
Your conversations become risk assessments.

And the tragedy compounds:
You long for someone to truly see you —
but you've hidden the real you so well
that even *you* don't know where to look.

Decision-making collapses next.

Without a solid self — without core values, private convictions, stable identity —

you don't choose based on what's right.
You choose based on what's *safe*.

Your moral compass no longer points north — it spins toward consensus.
You don't ask, *What matters?*
You ask, *What will they say?*

Even integrity becomes a variable.
Even ethics become fluid.
You become **strategic** instead of sincere.
And eventually, the line between action and manipulation disappears.

But here's the question that claws at the edge of all this performance:

> Can you come back?

Is redemption possible
after you've emptied yourself for applause?
Is there still a path back to the quiet self —
the one that wasn't optimized for approval,
but formed through wrestling, solitude, and truth?

The answer is terrifying and liberating:

Yes — but only through rupture.

The real self doesn't return through more applause.
It returns in the silence *after* the applause dies.
It comes when the image collapses.
When the mask cracks.
When you finally say something real — and lose people because of it.

> You cannot become whole while being everyone's favorite version of you.

Redemption begins not in reinvention,
but in **remembering** —
not who the world taught you to be,
but who you were before you learned to perform.

It is painful.
It is costly.
And it is your only way back.

Personas as Armor

The self we present to the world is almost never who we are.
It is who we *fear we need to be* to survive the eyes of others.

It is armor —
stitched together from childhood shame, social punishment, and the ever-tightening fear of exile.

We don't say,

> "This is what I believe."
> We ask,
> "How will this be received?"
> "Will this cost me approval?"
> "Will this offend the tribe?"

We pre-censor.
We pre-edit.
We pre-comply.

Because in an age of constant judgment, the **unfiltered self is a liability**.
So we sand ourselves down.
We chip away the inconvenient edges.
We replace conviction with calibration.

And slowly:
- We soften our opinions until they become echoes
- We conform our personality until it becomes product
- We delete our contradictions to avoid confusion
- We mute our instincts because rawness is threatening

And what's left is not a human being —
but an emotionally sanitized avatar.
A flattened, curated, hyper-palatable representation of "someone acceptable."

A walking PR campaign.
A carefully managed moral product.
A *self* so edited that not even we know what was cut out to make it safe.

And this armor works — at first.

It protects.
It earns applause.
It keeps the wolves away.

But it has a cost:

> **It doesn't just shield you from rejection — it buries you alive.**

You become so used to the mask that you forget how your real face feels.
You become fluent in self-preservation, but illiterate in authenticity.
You are never truly attacked —
but you are never truly *loved*, either.

Because no one can love a projection.
And no projection can evolve.
The persona is not built for growth.
It is built for survival.

And the more you survive, the less you live.

This is the paradox of performance:
The armor that shields your image will eventually **suffocate your soul**.

And here lies the final heartbreak:

> The persona becomes so convincing… even you believe it.
> You forget what it felt like to speak without flinching.
> You forget how it felt to say, "This is me," and mean it — even if no one clapped.

And by the time you realize what's missing,
you can't remember the last time you told the truth
without rehearsing it first.

The Loneliness of Performance

What most people call *burnout*
is often not the result of hard work —
but of **self-erasure**.

It is not your tasks that exhaust you.
It is the relentless, daily labor of *not being yourself*.
- Of pleasing.
- Of softening.
- Of anticipating offense.
- Of adjusting your language before your thoughts even form.

It's the **spiritual nausea** of never being alone —
even with yourself.

Because even in solitude, the crowd is in your head:

"Don't say that."
"That's too aggressive."
"That's problematic."
"Too privileged."
"Too emotional."
"Too nuanced."
"Too masculine."
"Too uneducated."
"Too much."

And so, with every decision, you rehearse.
With every word, you scan for risk.
With every truth, you consider its cost.

Eventually, you're not tired.
You're gone.

Case Study: The Activist Who Couldn't Say No

She was the face of the movement.
A voice for justice.
Unshakeable. Tireless.
Always showing up, always on fire, always "for the cause."

But privately:

- She felt **used**
- She disagreed with the group
- She craved **silence**, not spotlight

And yet, she kept posting.
She kept speaking.
She kept performing the character she had built from pieces of expectation.

Why?

Because her image had overtaken her soul.
She didn't know how to exit the stage without being called a **fraud**.

Her conscience was no longer private.
It was a **brand** — and the brand had to stay "on."

And so, like many who are applauded the loudest,
she disappeared.

Not in defiance.
Not in peace.
But in **psychic collapse**.

> She wasn't silenced.
> She was *emptied* — by the role she could no longer step out of.

How the Self Dies

The death of the self is not one moment.
It's not theatrical.
It's not loud.

It dies **quietly**.
In small, daily betrayals of truth.
- In the choice to "let it go" one more time
- In the twitch of discomfort you swallow to stay liked
- In the way your laughter gets softer, your beliefs more edited, your fire more manageable
- In the daily negotiation of what you're *allowed* to say
- In the growing space between what you feel and what you express

This is not maturity.
This is not diplomacy.
This is **moral self-dismantling**.

And the most terrifying part?

> You don't even notice it happening —
> until one day, someone asks,
> **"Who are you... when nobody is watching?"**

And you realize you have no answer.

Because the person who *could've answered*
is long gone —
edited, erased, applauded... and forgotten.

What We Lose

When the self disappears, so does everything that makes a life worth living.
You don't just lose identity. You lose:
• Conviction
• Courage
• Originality
• Spirituality
• True love
• Honest friendship
• And most devastating of all — the capacity to stand alone when the tribe is wrong

You become a **creature of reaction**. A shadow of other people's opinions. A vessel for whichever ideology pays the most attention.
You are no longer guided by your own compass, but dragged by tides you're too afraid to resist.
And so the human spirit becomes **morally plastic** — Shapeable. Discardable. Replaceable.
Because once a person becomes infinitely adjustable, infinitely agreeable, infinitely safe —
they are no longer a person at all.

The Neuroscience of Self-Suppression

The human brain was never meant to live like this.
It was not built to **self-monitor** with every breath. It cannot function under the constant pressure of social simulation.
And yet, this is our new default:
• Before we speak
• Before we feel
• Before we post We run a mental algorithm:

"Will this offend?" "Will this go viral for the wrong reason?" "Will they misunderstand me — and will that be survivable?"

This hypervigilance floods the nervous system with cortisol. It destabilizes the body. It erodes cognition.

The result?

- Chronic stress
- Dissociation
- Nervous exhaustion
- A brain that can no longer feel joy or speak truth without checking for applause first

When your nervous system is rewired for **survival-by-adjustment**, it loses the bandwidth for everything that makes you human:

- Creativity
- Integrity
- Spontaneity
- Love
- Peace

You're not living. You're **curating survival**.

Performance is Easier Than Authenticity

To live authentically is dangerous. It requires:

- Saying the unpopular thing
- Standing in contradiction
- Living in tension
- Owning your shadows — even when they horrify you

But *performance* is easier. It's cleaner. It offers insulation.

Instead of being brave, you become palatable. Instead of being whole, you become **digestible**.

And people love it.

They call you mature. They call you professional. They call you evolved. So you keep cutting off pieces of yourself — rough edges, controversial thoughts, inconvenient emotions — until all that remains is a sculpture that can pass any moral inspection.

But you don't just forget who you were.
You forget what got cut.
You forget what it felt like to speak with a full voice. You forget how to disagree without apologizing for existing. You forget that you once had a soul that burned — not to belong, but to be *true*.

Workplace Culture and the Professional Disappearance

Nowhere does the self vanish faster than inside a corporate mission statement.

Modern workplaces are the theaters of moral performance — where the most dangerous kind of conformity is repackaged as empowerment.

You are told to:

- "Be authentic" — but only in ways that flatter the brand
- "Speak up" — but only if your opinion has already been approved
- "Lead with empathy" — but never direct it toward systemic critique

These are not invitations.
They are **scripted illusions of autonomy** —
carefully worded HR-mantras designed to make obedience feel like leadership.

And so we adapt.
We shape-shift into corporate archetypes that look progressive, feel dynamic, and say absolutely nothing dangerous.

We roleplay:

- The "visionary" who disrupts nothing
- The "collaborator" who never disagrees
- The "resilient, empowered changemaker" who doesn't change a thing

We talk in mission statements.
We think in brand values.

We offer "feedback" that has already been sterilized for safe consumption.

> And all the while, a slow death is happening beneath the surface.

Because we are not collaborating.
We are **complying**.

We are not innovating.
We are **performing the simulation of innovation** — while being punished for original thought.

The modern work-self is a **ghost**:
- Always smiling
- Always available
- Always adjusting
- Never resisting
- Never resting
- Never *real*

Every word is pre-cleared.
Every emotion is repackaged.
Every act of resistance is turned into a "growth opportunity" — and then quietly buried.

We are told to bring our "whole selves" to work.
But what they really want is your compliant self,
your marketable self,
your non-threatening, emotionally intelligent, never-offending, always-aligned self.

And so, over time, you forget how to be anyone else.

You don't just lose your voice.
You **volunteer its extinction** — one "team-building" exercise at a time.

You no longer notice the betrayal because the betrayal has been normalized.
Packaged in slide decks.
Rewarded in performance reviews.
Celebrated in wellness webinars while your soul quietly dies in a browser tab.

This is not professionalism.
This is **institutionalized identity laundering** —
where your humanity is cleansed of its complexity,
your morality is filtered through profit metrics,
and your autonomy is converted into content.

The final tragedy?

> No one notices your disappearance.
> Because the version of you that remains still knows how to smile on Zoom.

Modern Parenting and the Pathologizing of the Real Self

The erosion doesn't start in adulthood.
It begins in childhood — now **engineered for performance**.

Even the earliest years are no longer protected from image management.
Children are:
- Diagnosed for emotional intensity
- Disciplined for spontaneity
- Coached for resilience before they've even formed their own desire
- Taught to speak like HR interns by the age of twelve

They grow up not asking, *"Who am I?"*
but learning to ask, *"Who do they need me to be?"*

And so by the time they reach adulthood, they don't rebel.
They **self-negotiate**.

The child disappears — not in trauma, but in *polished obedience*.
Not through abuse, but through over-guided, well-meaning, image-driven parenting.

They don't act out.
They perform serenity.
They say all the right things — while **dissociating beneath the applause**.

And by then, even *authenticity* is fake.

We're told:

>"Just be yourself."
>"Be raw."

"Be real."
"Be vulnerable."

But only if it photographs well.
Only if it performs.
Only if it *aligns with the moment and monetizes cleanly.*

Real authenticity would mean:
- Messiness
- Contradiction
- Anger
- Silence
- Regression
- Doubt
- Mystery

But that's not marketable.
So we're given *pre-approved scripts for healing*:
branded vulnerability, photogenic pain, monetized introspection.

> We don't become ourselves.
> We become **characters performing self-acceptance** —
> filtered through ring lights and captioned in lowercase emotionality.

It's not healing.
It's branding with tears.
It's the illusion of wholeness… sold as a lifestyle.

And here is the most chilling truth:

When the self disappears, what's left isn't peace —
It's **hollowness**.

You still wake up.
You still smile.
You still answer emails and post supportively.
But somewhere beneath it all, you feel like **someone else is living your life.**

- You don't recognize your own voice
- You feel slightly outside your body during every conversation
- You forget what you actually care about
- You dread being alone — not because it's quiet, but because you're not sure **there's anyone left in there**

This isn't depression.
It's **existential dislocation**.

Not sadness.
Absence.

And the world doesn't end when the self dies.

> It just becomes unbearable to live inside.

Final Reflection

The tragedy of the disappearing self is not loud. It doesn't come with crisis. It comes with **approval**.
It is not mourned. It is **rewarded**.
You'll get followers. You'll get promotions. You'll be praised for your professionalism, your adaptability, your emotional intelligence.
And maybe you *are* succeeding.

Maybe you've become the person they wanted you to be.
But every day, a voice inside you grows a little quieter — the one that once whispered,

"This isn't me." "This isn't what I believe." "This isn't who I was supposed to become."

And if you ignore it long enough, it doesn't scream. It just stops speaking. Not out of surrender — but because it knows no one's listening anymore. Not even you.

And all that's left is:
- A role.
- A script.
- A well-managed shell with excellent optics and no soul.

The world will love you. But **you will be gone**.

Case Study: Corporate DEI Training Programs

The modern workplace is no longer where you work. It's where you **perform identity**.

Mandatory "inclusion" training becomes behavioral programming — telling you how to think, speak, and "show up" in morally safe ways. Not to build understanding — but to **standardize conscience**.

Real diversity — of thought, experience, contradiction, doubt — is not welcomed. It is quietly removed. Those who ask hard questions are seen not as complex, but as *threats*.

So people stop asking. They say the right things. They signal the right virtues.

And what remains is not a self — but a **scripted persona** who has learned to look empathetic while feeling nothing.

The disappearance is complete. Not because anyone forced it. But because it was easier. Because it paid well. Because no one told you it was happening — until it was too late to stop.

And now you live with a version of yourself that never says the wrong thing, never offends, never stands too tall.

A version the world rewards.

But not one it will remember. And not one *you* will recognize when you're alone with yourself.

❖❖❖

Chapter 13

THE WAR ON REALITY

"When truth becomes offensive, we replace it with narrative."

Truth Is Now Violence. Narrative Is Now Virtue

There was a time when truth stood outside of us.

It didn't care how we felt.
It didn't soften its tone to spare our identity.
It simply was.

But in the modern age, truth is treated as aggression.
It is labeled dangerous, harmful, triggering, unsafe.

> Not because it's false —
> but because it refuses to flatter the story we want to tell.

So we rewrite the rules.
We replace **truth** with **narrative**,
evidence with **experience**,
biology with **identity**,
reality with *whatever gets the most applause*.

And we call it compassion.
We call it justice.
We call it *progress* — even as it quietly unravels the foundations of sanity.

Today:

- A man can be punished for stating a biological fact
- A woman can be erased for protecting the definition of the word
- A scientist can be censored for publishing inconvenient data
- A child can be taught that feelings override anatomy, and to question that is "hate"

This isn't cultural evolution.
This is **epistemological collapse** —
a world where truth no longer matters unless it *performs well*.

And the most disturbing part?

> This was not forced upon us.
> We volunteered for it.

We chose emotional safety over cognitive integrity.
We chose tribal applause over uncomfortable facts.
We chose to feel righteous — not *to be right*.

And so, we began calling anything that unsettled us "harmful."
And anything that confirmed our identity "true."

Reality didn't become less real.
We just **rewired our language to hide from it.**

This is not kindness.
This is delusion, professionally curated and morally framed.

We are not advancing.
We are *unmooring*.

Because if reality is whatever we declare it to be,
then morality isn't a compass —
it's a **costume department.**

The Masculinity Crisis

Masculinity today is not simply under question —
it is **under siege**.

Not just by feminism, but by a deeper, more corrosive force:
moral confusion masquerading as progress.

We have reached a cultural moment where to be male is to be *guilty by default*,
where natural masculine traits are **not only discouraged, but pathologized** —
framed as threats to civility, equality, and emotional safety.

Let's be clear:

- **Boys are raised without fathers** in staggering numbers — a reality with measurable effects on emotional regulation, school performance, and long-term identity formation.
- **Masculine instincts** — risk-taking, physical assertiveness, emotional stoicism, competitive drive — are now labeled as "toxic," not because they are inherently harmful, but because they contradict the **cultural script of vulnerability as virtue.**
- And when boys become men, they are given a contradictory checklist of moral compliance:

Be strong, but soft.
Be assertive, but deferential.
Be stoic, but emotionally fluent.
Be protective, but never patriarchal.
Lead — but only when given permission.

This is not guidance.
This is **psychological sabotage**.

Because when a man fails to live up to these impossible standards, he is mocked for being weak.
When he succeeds in traditional strength, he is feared or demonized.
And if he dares to **resist** the moral script,
he is *publicly shamed, digitally erased, or institutionally punished.*

This isn't balance.
This is identity gaslighting at scale.

And boys are internalizing the confusion.

They are learning not to harness their instincts,
but to **apologize for having them**.

They are taught to:
- Suppress ambition as "toxic capitalism"
- Swallow discomfort to avoid appearing fragile
- Abandon competitiveness in the name of equality
- Sit quietly in classrooms designed for verbal processing and emotional compliance
- Absorb the message that they are "privileged oppressors" — even as they **fall behind in education, mental health, marriage, and life expectancy**

Real-world data backs this collapse:
- Men now make up less than 40% of university graduates across most Western countries
- Male suicide rates are **3 to 4 times higher** than female rates globally
- Marriage rates and fatherhood involvement are plummeting, while loneliness and porn addiction are rising
- Testosterone levels in men have dropped by over **30% in the past 40 years**, with no biological cause to explain the change aside from environmental and behavioral factors

This is not cultural evolution.
This is **biological deprogramming** disguised as moral sensitivity.

We are not raising more emotionally intelligent men.
We are **producing fragile, ashamed, disoriented shells** of what boys

might have become
had they been told that masculinity is not a flaw — but a force to be cultivated with discipline and purpose.

And here lies the true crisis:

> Masculinity hasn't disappeared.
> It's been **shamed into exile.**

What we've created is not progress,
but a generation of young men who feel both *unwanted and morally condemned.*

They are **lonely, confused, directionless**, and deeply suspicious of the cultural institutions that claim to care about them.

And when the culture offers no dignified role for their strength,
no path for their risk-taking,
no outlet for their ambition —
they will go looking elsewhere.

Some turn inward and disappear.
Others turn outward and burn things down.

And then we act surprised.

Feminism's New Costume: Control Through Fragility

First-wave feminism fought for dignity.
Second-wave feminism fought for opportunity.
But the modern wave no longer fights for liberation —
it fights for **dominance through fragility**.

It wears the language of justice,
but it operates through **moral coercion** —
not to create balance,
but to **centralize emotional power.**

The sacred word was and is still *equality*, and now combined with equity - but the mechanisms are pure control:

- **Control over language** — Say "woman" instead of "womxn," refuse the label "cis," question a single ideological narrative, and you are instantly recast not as mistaken, but as *unsafe*.
- **Control over space** — Your very **presence** as a man can now be interpreted as a threat. No action required. Your existence triggers accusation.
- **Control over power** — Any difference in outcome, any expression of strength, even assertiveness in tone — is framed not as diversity, but as *oppression*.

This is not empowerment.
This is **emotional imperialism** —
the colonization of public and private spaces through weaponized sensitivity.

Women are now framed as **two things at once**:
- Empowered, fearless, evolved, morally superior

- And simultaneously fragile, wounded, silenced, and perpetually under assault

This paradox is not accidental.
It is a **strategy**.

Because it creates a condition where every interaction is pre-loaded with guilt — and only one side gets to define the rules.

If you question the narrative, you're oppressive.
If you assert your own, you're violent.
If you ask for clarity, you're "gaslighting."

Modern feminism, in its most performative form, doesn't ask for dialogue.
It demands **submission** — disguised as solidarity.

The message to men is clear:

"You are the threat.
You are the obstacle.
You are the problem."

But the message to women is **even more sinister**:

*"You are a victim — unless you control the narrative.
You are powerful — only when you dominate the emotional terrain."*

This is no longer about female empowerment.
It is **identity-based moral weaponization**.

It replaces universal dignity with tribal grievance.
It replaces mutual respect with ideological choreography.
And it replaces the radical complexity of real womanhood
with a performance template of who women must now be:

- Fierce, but wounded
- Unapologetic, but offended
- Superior, but persecuted
- In charge — but always emotionally at risk

And anything less than total affirmation of this dynamic is labeled as violence, misogyny, or erasure.

This is not feminism.
This is **a cultural hostage crisis**
draped in progressive language,
where freedom is redefined as **obedience to the script.**

And everyone — men and women alike —
knows something is wrong,
but **no one dares say it**,
for fear of being *corrected, shamed, or erased.*

DEI: The Cult of Appearances

Diversity. Equity. Inclusion. Three words that began with noble intent — now hollowed out, rebranded, and deployed as **ideological performance art**.

In theory, DEI promised fairness. In practice, it now delivers **fear-based compliance**.

Because DEI today doesn't measure outcomes or opportunity. It measures **optics, obedience, and performative remorse**.

It champions:
- Diversity of skin — but not thought
- Equity of outcomes — not access
- Inclusion — for everyone who already agrees

This isn't justice. It's **bureaucratized moral theater** — where appearance is everything, and truth is a liability.

It creates:
- **Token hires** — where difference is decorative, not substantive
- **Reverse discrimination** — where merit is sacrificed to meet quotas that flatter the brand
- **Compliance culture** — where people speak in code to avoid triggering the latest emotional landmine
- **Workplace mistrust** — where every meeting is a minefield, every question is suspect, every silence is politically loaded

And the worst outcome?

It punishes **authenticity**.

You're no longer a human being. You're a **representative category**. Your words are no longer heard. They are filtered through **identity optics**:
- If you speak out, you're labeled divisive.
- If you question the premise, you're unsafe.
- If you stay silent, you're complicit.

This is not inclusion. It is **emotional hostage-taking**.

Emotional Blackmail as Moral Currency

The DEI-industrial complex is not built on data. It is built on **emotional coercion** — the subtle threat that to question is to kill.

You've heard it:
- "If you don't support this, people will die."
- "If you push back, you're the reason for suicide."
- "If you question this framework, you're a threat to safety."

This is not conversation. This is **weaponized empathy.**

It replaces argument with accusation. It turns genuine disagreement into psychological violence. It uses trauma as a **moral bludgeon** — not to seek healing, but to enforce conformity.

And here's the most chilling twist:

Real victims exist. Real injustice matters. But when victimhood becomes **currency**, the economy becomes corrupt.

You're not allowed to:
- Ask for evidence
- Acknowledge nuance
- Weigh competing interests
- Explore unintended consequences

Because to do so is to "harm." To explore complexity is to "invalidate." To seek balance is to "erase."

And so we collapse the entire framework of reason.

We create a false equivalence between questioning and violence. Between logic and bigotry. Between disagreement and *harm*.

This is not progress. This is a **moral racket** — a system where outrage replaces proof, and silence is demanded in the name of "allyship."

And in that silence, something precious dies:

Not just free speech. Not just intellectual honesty. But **the very idea of truth itself.**

The Indoctrination of Children

The war on reality doesn't begin in adulthood. It begins in the classroom. Children are no longer taught how to think. They are taught **what to feel** — and more importantly, *who to blame*.

They are handed pre-packaged identities and moral scripts before they've developed curiosity, autonomy, or emotional resilience.

They are told:
- "Gender is a choice."
- "Sex is a social construct."
- "Truth is oppressive."
- "Discomfort is trauma."
- "Disagreement is harm."

This is not education. This is **psychological grooming** — not sexual, but ideological — to see the world through the lens of **fragility, grievance, and curated identity.**

They're not given tools. They're given roles:
- "You're non-binary."
- "You're an oppressor."
- "You're a victim."
- "You're unsafe around people who disagree with you."

And so, the classroom becomes a **stage for moral pageantry** — where the currency is outrage, and the highest grade is ideological alignment. This is not empowerment. It's **indoctrination through emotional scripting**. And the result is not liberation — but confusion, narcissism, fragility, and eventually: **rage**.

Because these children are not taught how to navigate reality. They're taught how to *perform* it — under constant surveillance, with moral applause as the reward for compliance.

And underneath it all, language itself is collapsing.

Words no longer mean what they meant. They now serve ideological function, not clarity:
- "Woman" means anyone who says so
- "Diversity" means everyone who agrees
- "Violence" means dissent
- "Justice" means revenge
- "Empathy" means obedience
- "Safety" means silence from the other side

This is not evolution. This is **semantic decay** — a deliberate erosion of meaning so that language becomes *a weapon, not a bridge*.

Because once **meaning becomes subjective**, truth becomes irrelevant. And once truth dies, all that remains is **power** — enforced not through evidence, but through:
- Guilt
- Shame
- Cancellation
- Fear

We are not just losing words. We are losing the **capacity to think independently**.

Because thought requires structure. Structure requires language. And when language becomes moral propaganda, thinking becomes emotional obedience.

And without the ability to think, what we call "identity" is nothing more than a **costume** — approved by committee, updated by consensus, and discarded when the trend shifts.

Final Reflection

Reality does not fight back.
It doesn't scream when rewritten.
It doesn't plead when replaced by narrative.
It simply **withdraws** —
and waits for us to feel the consequences.

We tell ourselves we are evolving.
That we are becoming more inclusive, more sensitive, more advanced.

But beneath the slogans, beneath the applause,
something ancient and irreplaceable is vanishing:

- A shared language.
- A common truth.
- A stable identity.
- A coherent self.

And in its place, we are left with **fragile ideologies dressed in moral costumes**.
We are left with children who can't distinguish discomfort from oppression.
With adults who mistake emotion for argument.
With institutions built not on excellence or truth — but on fear.

And the final illusion is the most seductive:

> That we can build a better world **by erasing reality**.

But you cannot delete biology without consequence.
You cannot rewrite language without confusion.
You cannot abolish truth and expect sanity to survive.

What follows is not utopia.
It is **disorientation**, masked as progress.

It is **obedience**, framed as empathy.
It is **collapse**, choreographed as virtue.

And when it finally comes undone —
when the narratives fracture,
when the contradictions become unbearable,
when the mirror turns and there is no one behind it —

> We will look for something real to hold.
> And realize we burned it long ago —
> **because it made us uncomfortable.**

Chapter 14

THE CULT OF THE GOOD PERSON

"They'll never raise their voice — but they will erase you."

The Rise of the Harmless Hero

In today's culture, the highest compliment is no longer *"wise," "brave,"* or *"honest."*

It's:

"Nice."
"Kind."
"Safe."

Virtue has been de-fanged.
Moral greatness has been traded for **emotional warmth**.
We don't worship saints or thinkers anymore.
We worship **non-threatening personalities.**

The ideal citizen is now:
- Agreeable
- Apologetic
- Endlessly inclusive
- Smooth at all social angles
- Emotionally available but *never* morally polarizing

They will never raise their voice.
They will never draw a line.
They will never say anything sharp, true, or difficult that might cause friction.

They will use all the right phrases.
They will validate every identity.
They will nod along with whatever the dominant moral trend happens to be this week —
even if it contradicts last week.

They are adored.
Not for their courage — but for their **compliance with comfort.**

But beneath this soft exterior lies something far more insidious.

Because this "harmless hero" is not humble.
They are **morally vain** —
so obsessed with being seen as good, so allergic to confrontation, that they will **destroy anyone who disturbs their image of themselves**.

They don't punish with fists.
They punish with silence.
With removal.
With polite distancing, public shaming, and passive-aggressive correctness.

They are not cruel in tone.
They are **surgical in effect.**

They speak in the voice of empathy,
but wield the tools of **social execution**.

They'll smile as they erase you.
They'll post about compassion while reporting your disagreement.
They'll praise dialogue while silencing dissent.

This is not goodness.
It is **emotional authoritarianism** in a cardigan.
It is virtue as **emotional camouflage** — weaponized through community standards and corporate slogans.

And most people never see it.
Because it doesn't scream.
It *performs concern*.

And in a world trained to equate kindness with morality, the person who never offends becomes untouchable — and unaccountable.

They've become the new sacred figure:
Not because they are strong, but because they are **inoffensive**.
Not because they protect truth, but because they protect *comfort*.

And that makes them the perfect soldier for the soft totalitarianism of modern virtue:
- Polite
- Pleasant
- Deadly

Weaponized Niceness: When Kindness Kills

Niceness has become the new morality —
not truth, not justice, not courage.

And in this new order, the most dangerous people are not the loud bigots or obvious abusers.
They are the ones who use **kindness as a weapon** —
soft, clean, and lethal.

These are the people who say:
- "I just want to make sure everyone feels safe."
- "Let's not be negative."
- "That kind of tone isn't helpful."
- "Can we all just be respectful?"
- "It's not what you said — it's how it made people feel."

On the surface, these sound virtuous.
But underneath is a silent decree:

> "Stop being uncomfortable. Or we'll remove you."

In this world, **truth becomes rudeness**, and honesty becomes violence.
- Tell an uncomfortable fact? You're "abrasive."
- Ask for evidence? You're "invalidating."
- Hold the line on principle? You're "unsafe to work with."

This isn't kindness.
It's emotional censorship with a smile.

These "good people" don't debate you — they **de-platform** you.
They don't argue — they **isolate**.
They don't scream — they **send HR emails**.

And when you're gone, they'll light a candle, post a quote about "healing," and tell the world how painful it was to lose someone "so out of alignment."

They never break the rules.
They simply change the rules
until **you no longer fit inside them.**

And the brilliance of it all?

> The attack is invisible.
> The weapon is **niceness itself.**

No one sees the violence because it's done with concern.
No one sees the manipulation because it's wrapped in mindfulness and emotional language.

It's not "cancel culture," they'll say — it's **protecting community energy.**
It's not exile — it's "setting boundaries."
It's not erasure — it's "curating safe space."

But the result is always the same:
- A voice silenced
- A conscience punished
- A truth buried
- A soul edited out of the room

And all of it done by "good people" doing their best.

The Psychology of the Good Person

The "good person" is not driven by malice. They are driven by something far more insidious: the unrelenting need to be seen as good.

This craving is not shallow. It is existential. Being perceived as moral isn't just a preference — it's their identity.

Their sense of worth, of safety, of self, depends entirely on remaining untarnished in the eyes of the tribe. And so, anything that threatens that image — disagreement, contradiction, challenge — is experienced not as an opportunity for growth, but as an existential threat. Dissent becomes danger. Discomfort becomes violence. And truth becomes too costly to keep.

This is why the good person cannot debate. Debate implies uncertainty. They cannot handle contradiction, because contradiction implies complexity, and complexity threatens coherence.

They cannot be disagreed with, because disagreement introduces the possibility that they are not wholly good — and that is a reality they cannot emotionally tolerate. So instead of wrestling with the possibility of being wrong, they outsource their morality to the cultural script.

They memorize the slogans, repeat the approved phrases, wear the right badges, and surround themselves with mirrors that reflect their moral glow back at them. They perform virtue fluently, but only within the limits of what is safe.

Their empathy is rehearsed. Their kindness is curated. Their conscience is shaped entirely by what the dominant culture finds palatable this month. They never question gender ideology.

They never push back on DEI orthodoxy. They never raise concerns about victim-centered politics or emotional blackmail disguised as activism. Not because they deeply believe — but because questioning would feel impolite. And in the gospel of the good person, impoliteness is the new heresy.

They are not brave. But they are perfectly aligned. They are moral conformists dressed as empathic citizens. They stand for everything — as long as everything is emotionally safe, socially reinforced, and conflict-free.

Their version of morality is not forged in fire, but shaped in group chats and HR seminars. And when you disrupt their comfort, they won't yell. They won't argue. They won't tell you you're wrong. They'll just disappear you.

They will unfollow. Uninvite. Avoid. They'll ghost you and call it emotional safety. They'll say they're "protecting their peace" while making sure you're no longer allowed to speak in the room.

They'll let the tribe do the canceling, while they maintain the appearance of calm civility. They are the velvet glove of modern morality — and the sharpest blade.

And they genuinely believe they're being kind. They will go to sleep convinced they are compassionate, tolerant, and loving — even as they leave behind a trail of erased friendships, silent excommunications, and reputations destroyed through omission. They don't burn books. They just stop inviting the authors. They don't stone heretics. They just politely delete them from the feed.

This is not virtue. This is emotional cowardice repackaged as goodness. It is moral performance without moral substance. It is obedience to a script that requires no backbone, only bandwidth. It is the death of character — done gently, sweetly, and always with a smile.

Institutionalizing the Good

In today's institutions—corporations, schools, NGOs, media—the "good person" is no longer just celebrated. They are **installed**. They are **institutionalized**. They become the new blueprint for who is allowed to lead, who is allowed to speak, and ultimately, who is allowed to exist inside the system.

They know the rules: say the right things, use the approved language, emote in all the correct ways, ask no hard questions, and most of all—be emotionally validating at all times. Their talent is not brilliance. It's **compliance masquerading as virtue**. They do not disturb. They do not create. They do not contradict. They ascend because they fit the architecture of modern moral bureaucracy perfectly.

These are the people who rise—fast.

They become your HR directors, your communications leads, your ethics officers, your wellness managers, your DEI consultants. Not because they have depth, or courage, or vision—but because they are **emotionally frictionless**. They are perfectly engineered to reflect the moral anxieties of the institution back to itself in soothing language. They reduce all disagreement to "tone." They turn policy into therapy. They mistake safety for growth.

And from these positions of influence, they begin to quietly **rewrite the moral code** of the entire institution.

Truth becomes secondary to tone.
Evidence becomes less important than empathy.
Excellence is sacrificed for emotional alignment.
Debate becomes dangerous.
Discomfort becomes taboo.
Dissent becomes trauma.

And the institution itself becomes a performance space.
Not for work.
Not for learning.
Not for exploration.
But for **continuous emotional signaling**.

Everyone learns the lesson quickly:
If you want to survive, **mirror the script**.
If you want to succeed, **feel the right things**—or at least appear to.

And so, the culture hardens into a kind of moral monoculture—
self-policing, self-censoring, self-reinforcing.

Not because anyone is being explicitly silenced,
but because everyone has absorbed the same invisible directive:

> **Don't make anyone uncomfortable.**
> **Don't be real.**
> **Be good.**

And when institutions become temples to niceness,
when "being good" means "being agreeable,"
truth dies—not with violence,
but with **a standing ovation**.

Why the Good Person is Dangerous

The good person doesn't lie.
They just refuse to look at the truth if it's painful.
They don't hate you.
They just drift away the moment your beliefs become socially risky.
They don't seek power.
But they end up with it—because in today's world, **power flows to those who best perform moral optics.**

They don't silence you violently.
They simply **erase your voice through absence**.
Through disapproval. Through polite exclusion. Through quiet abandonment.

They never meant harm.
They wanted peace. Belonging. Approval.
They wanted to be seen as someone good, someone kind, someone pure.

But in their relentless pursuit of being *untouchable*, they became:
- Blind to truth
- Deaf to complexity
- Hostile to courage
- Addicted to applause

And worst of all, they helped build a world where **no one can afford to be real**—because being real might make someone uncomfortable. And in a culture where discomfort is the new violence, truth itself becomes unlivable.

They are not villains.
They are **mirrors**—of our fear, our silence, our survival instincts dressed up as values.

They are what we all become when we worship belonging more than integrity.

And that is what makes them the **final obstacle before truth can return.**
Not because they are malicious.
But because they are morally anesthetized.

They will cry for causes.
They will post for victims.
They will light digital candles and write poetic captions about how "heartbroken" they are after every global tragedy.

They'll change their profile picture.
They'll say the right thing.
They'll prove how deeply they care—**publicly, visibly, socially.**

But nothing follows.
No action. No sacrifice. No internal reckoning.

Because the grief was never for justice.
It was for identity.
It wasn't mourning—it was **emotional cosplay**.

A performance of compassion to signal tribal alignment.
A safe display of sadness to prove:

> *"I am one of the good ones."*

And in the echo chamber of curated virtue, **performative grief becomes social currency,** not a catalyst for anything real.

They don't want transformation.
They want comfort.
They want inclusion.

They want to feel righteous without doing the dangerous work of righteousness.

So when the real moment comes—when truth would cost them something, when integrity requires dissent, when courage means stepping outside the tribe—they say:
- "I don't want drama."
- "Let's just stay positive."
- "Now's not the time."
- "Let's not divide people."
- "Can't we just focus on what unites us?"

These are not peacekeeping phrases.
They are **deflection mechanisms**.
Moral camouflage for **cowardice in a nice tone of voice**.

They allow the "good person" to:
- Avoid hard truths
- Evade moral courage
- Stay comfortable while others are sacrificed

This is how **niceness becomes a moral alibi**.
How softness becomes silence.
How kindness becomes complicity.

And how the world slowly descends into moral delusion—guided not by tyrants, but by nice people with nothing to lose and no truth they're willing to die for.

The Ethics of Silence

The good person doesn't lie when truth becomes dangerous.
They just go quiet.

They say, *"I'm staying out of it."*
They frame their silence as neutrality.
As peacekeeping.
As maturity.

But in doing so, they:

- Leave the truth undefended
- Allow injustice to metastasize
- Reward conformity over conscience
- And protect their moral image from the social cost of dissent

They call it "respecting both sides."
They say it's about "choosing peace."
They insist they're just "being emotionally safe."

But underneath all of it is fear.
Not fear of harm — fear of **discomfort**.
Fear of being misread.
Fear of being unliked.
Fear of losing access to the tribe.

Because for the good person, being seen as good is more important than being good.

And this is exactly why the archetype spreads.
The good person thrives in environments where **image matters more than truth**:

- Schools
- HR departments

- Media companies
- Nonprofits
- Universities

These are not arenas of rigorous thought anymore.
They are theaters of moral appearance.
Places where discomfort is considered harm, and emotional sensitivity becomes a form of unchallengeable authority.

In these spaces:
- Conformity is praised
- Niceness is rewarded
- Truth is filtered through what is least likely to upset anyone

And soon, entire systems are no longer run by truth-seekers —
but by **emotional consensus managers**,
whose job is not to pursue what's real,
but to punish what disrupts the illusion of harmony.

The good person doesn't become dangerous because they hate truth.
They become dangerous because **truth creates tension** —
and tension threatens the performance of their identity.

So they:
- Censor without calling it censorship
- Marginalize disagreement under the banner of "care"
- Equate discomfort with danger
- And slowly create an environment where only the **curated self** is allowed to survive

They don't raise their voice — but they will remove yours.
They won't argue — but they will disappear when you fall.
They don't say it aloud — but deep down, they believe **their comfort is worth more than your truth**.

And that is how the world collapses quietly:
Not through tyranny, but through **moral softness weaponized into silence.**

Final Reflection

The good person was not born evil.
They were born into a culture that rewards **optics over integrity**.
They didn't invent the mask.
They just wore it so convincingly,
they forgot it wasn't skin.

They don't see themselves as cowards.
They see themselves as kind.
As peaceful.
As emotionally safe.

But their kindness is calibrated for applause.
Their empathy is rehearsed.
Their silence is strategic.

They live not to do good,
but to be **seen** doing good.
To be **praised** for being safe.
To be **untouched** by the blood of hard truths.

They will never raise their voice.
They will never throw the first stone.
They will just **step back quietly** and let the tribe do the work for them.

They are the nicest people you'll ever meet.
And they will destroy you — gently.

Not because they want to hurt you.
But because **your presence disrupts the script** they've spent their lives performing.

And in a world that confuses peace with performance,
that alone is unforgivable.

Case Study: The Silent Social Circle

A friend shares a controversial opinion.
Not hateful. Not cruel.
Just *nonconforming*.

The group chat goes quiet.
No one argues.
No one defends.
They just… stop responding.

The air shifts.
A polite exile begins.

No accusations are made.
No lines are drawn.
Just fewer invites.
Fewer mentions.
Fewer replies.

And within weeks, the person is gone.
Not attacked.
Not debated.
Just **socially erased**.

The "good people" didn't cancel them.
They just disappeared when it was no longer convenient to care.

Their virtue wasn't in what they did.
It was in *what they avoided*.
Their morality wasn't in courage —
but in **never being near discomfort**.

And in a culture where silence protects reputation more than truth ever could,
this is what passes for goodness now.

Chapter 15

A MIRROR INSTEAD OF A FLAG

"You don't need to agree. You just need to be honest."

What This Book Was Never Meant to Be

This book was never meant to make you feel safe.

It was not written for agreement, or belonging, or applause.
It was not designed to flatter your tribe, comfort your worldview, or help you role-play a more enlightened version of yourself.
It is not "for" the left. It is not "for" the right. It is not "for" centrists.
It is not for good people. It is not for bad people.
It is for people who are *done pretending*.

This book was never meant to be part of the performance.
It was written to **burn the stage down.**

If you came looking for solutions, you won't find them.
If you came hoping to feel morally superior, you won't.
If you're still here expecting to be validated, stop reading now.

Because this book does not offer safety.
It offers a **reckoning**.

A reckoning with how far we've drifted from anything real.
A reckoning with what we've allowed ourselves to become in the name of virtue.
A reckoning with the cheap applause we trade for conscience.
A reckoning with the masks we wear so long we forget what our real face feels like underneath.

This book was never meant to give you something to wave.
It was meant to give you something to *face*.

Not a flag.
Not a tribe.
Not a role.
A **mirror**.

Because the truth is: we don't need more slogans.
We don't need more moral posturing, or curated grief, or branded humility.
We don't need another list of "right things to say."

What we need—what we've always needed—is something terrifying:

> A moment of **unfiltered honesty**, without applause, without strategy, without audience.

This book has no heroes.
No villains.
No saviors.
Just people.

Flawed. Fragile. Self-deceiving.
And capable of **extraordinary clarity** when the illusions finally fall away.

So no—this book was never meant to be liked.
It was meant to **leave a mark**.

And if you've made it here,
then some part of you knows:

> You are not who the crowd thinks you are.
> And you are ready—finally—to stop acting.

The Cost of the Lie

The lie we live isn't shouted.
It's whispered.
Daily.
Internally.
Quiet enough to ignore, loud enough to rot us from the inside.

It sounds like:

> "Just don't say that here."
> "It's not worth the conflict."
> "Keep it to yourself — they wouldn't understand."
> "Now's not the time."
> "Just nod along and get through it."

We tell ourselves we're being mature.
Respectful.
Professional.
Empathetic.

But really, we are **negotiating with our own conscience** —
selling off pieces of our integrity in exchange for emotional safety.

And it works.
At first.

The silence protects you.
The smile keeps you included.
The moral script earns you nods, followers, friends.
You're called good. Thoughtful. Emotionally intelligent.

But the cost isn't what they see.
The cost is what **you stop being able to feel.**

Every time you lie by omission, something numbs.
Every time you play along, something fades.

Every time you perform a belief you don't hold, something **fractures** inside you.

And eventually, the fractures connect.

Until one day:
- You don't know what you think anymore.
- You don't know what you believe unless the group tells you.
- You don't speak truth — you simulate consensus.
- You don't even remember what it felt like to be **unfiltered and whole**.

This is the hidden toll.
The psychological erosion that doesn't make headlines or hashtags.

> It's not that you disappear all at once.
> It's that you slowly become **a ghost of yourself** —
> Someone who's still smiling, still belonging, still posting…
> but utterly hollow.

You don't lose your job.
You lose your voice.

You don't lose your friends.
You lose your ability to speak honestly in front of them.

You don't lose your mind.
You lose your **inner life** —
replaced by a loop of moral simulation, always calculating the safest thing to say.

This is the cost of the lie:
Not death.
Not exile.

But **emotional anesthesia** —
the slow, silent death of truth in the name of goodness.

And when the mask finally cracks,
you'll find you've forgotten how to speak in your own voice.

You Are Not Innocent — and That's the Point

If you've made it this far and still believe you're one of the "good ones," you weren't reading — you were scanning for confirmation.

Because here's the truth:

> **You are not innocent.**
> And you were never meant to be.

You've been silent when it mattered.
You've nodded at lies.
You've rewarded performance.
You've punished honesty — in others and in yourself.

You've posted what was expected.
You've apologized for things you didn't believe.
You've sat in rooms where truth was absent, and said nothing — because you were tired, or scared, or wanted to be liked.

You've watched someone be exiled for being real —
and did nothing.
Or worse: you clapped.

And still, the world called you good.

Because you were nice.
Because you were safe.

Because you made people feel comfortable — even as something in you twisted with the knowledge that **comfort was bought with silence**.

But this isn't an indictment.

This is a **release**.

Because the goal of this book was never to leave you drowning in shame.
It was to show you that your **innocence was the illusion**,
and your participation was the price of being allowed to belong.

You were never asked to be real.
You were asked to be **harmless**.
And you learned to be so good at surviving the script that you forgot it was a script at all.

But that's the point.

You're not a villain.
You're not even unique.

You are what the system **trained you to become**:
Adaptable. Pleasing. Morally presentable.
Someone who knows how to survive in a world that rewards image over integrity.

And that's why you're not condemned.
You're *free*.

> Free to stop pretending.
> Free to step off the stage.
> Free to be **flawed, uncertain, messy — and finally, human again**.

You will not be pure.
You will not be applauded.
You will not be safe.

But you will be **real**.

And real is the only place truth can live.

The Way Out Isn't Heroism — It's Reality

There is no speech to give.
No group to join.
No identity to reclaim.
There is no applause waiting on the other side of your honesty.

> The way out isn't heroic.
> It's **quiet. Private. Unmarketable.**

It starts not with some grand act of defiance,
but with a moment — maybe this one —
where you say, without irony,

> *"I don't believe what I've been pretending to believe."*

That's it.
The first tear in the costume.

The next step isn't dramatic either.
It's noticing how often you pause before you speak.
It's observing which truths you edit, and for whom.
It's hearing yourself say something performative — and feeling the wince.
It's realizing how many of your friendships depend on mutual moral acting.

And then slowly, without permission,
you begin to **choose truth over safety**.

You say less.
But when you speak, you mean it.
You stop rehearsing your empathy.
You stop laughing at jokes you don't agree with.
You stop agreeing out of fear.
You start saying, *"I don't know."*
You start saying, *"That's not true for me."*
You start telling the truth — not all the time, not perfectly, but **enough to feel the burn**.

This isn't about becoming loud.
It's about becoming **aligned**.

Not aligned with your tribe.
Aligned with **yourself**.

No hashtags.
No applause.
No flag to wave.

Just a quiet return to something **undeniably real**.
Something that existed before you learned how to perform.

You don't have to be brave.
You just have to stop lying.

We Don't Want Truth — We Want Roles

We say we want truth.
We don't.

What we really want is **a role**.
Something that tells us who to be, how to speak, what to feel, and when to clap.

Roles are safe.
Truth is dangerous.

Roles come with scripts.
Truth comes with consequences.

Roles give us tribe.
Truth might leave us **alone**.

So we don't pursue what's real.
We pursue **what will be approved.**

We'd rather be:
- The "activist"
- The "ally"
- The "truth-teller"
- The "healer"
- The "good man"
- The "kind woman"
- The "brave survivor"
- The "wellness warrior"
- The "righteous skeptic"
- The "empathic leader"

Even our rebellion becomes a costume.

We join identity groups not for truth, but for **prewritten significance**.
We outsource our depth to templates.
We don't become someone — we **adopt a brand**.

Because in a world where image is currency,
truth is too unpredictable.
It doesn't scale.
It doesn't monetize.
It doesn't always make people like you.

So we perform instead.
We curate.
We repeat the lines that come with the costume we've chosen.
And we call it a self.

But underneath the perfect persona,
beneath the emotional literacy and "safe space" vocabulary,
we are **starving** for something real.

Not applause.
Not followers.
Not moral high ground.

> *Just the raw, unfiltered freedom of saying:*
> *"I don't know who I am yet — but at least I'm not faking it anymore."*

That's the beginning of identity.
Everything before that was **roleplay**.

The Psychological Weight of Pretending

Pretending doesn't feel heavy at first.

It feels smart.
Strategic.
Socially aware.
You're adapting. Navigating. Getting along.

But pretending is not adaptation.
It's **self-abandonment**, done in small, daily doses.

And the weight builds slowly:
- That moment you smile when you disagree.
- That conversation you escape instead of tell the truth.
- That belief you silence because it might offend.
- That joke you laugh at so they'll keep including you.
- That post you make so they don't start asking questions.

None of it feels like betrayal.
Until you realize **you've betrayed yourself 400 times this year.**

And now:
- You feel tired when you're alone.
- You feel fake when you're with people.
- You don't know what's true or just "socially appropriate."
- You can't relax because performance never ends.
- You don't remember what it feels like to speak without editing yourself mid-sentence.

This isn't burnout.
It's **emotional fragmentation**.

You haven't lost energy.
You've just spent it all keeping your image alive.

Pretending is expensive.
It costs your aliveness.
It trades truth for survival, over and over, until your nervous system no longer knows what safety feels like unless it's *filtered through approval.*

You tell yourself you're being mature.
You're keeping the peace.
You're being professional.
You're being thoughtful.

But deep down, some part of you is screaming:

> *"I don't want to manage myself anymore just to be accepted."*

And maybe you've ignored that voice for years.
Maybe you buried it in spiritual language, political alignment, or workplace etiquette.
But the body keeps the truth.
And the soul keeps score.

Pretending is not sustainable.
It doesn't break you overnight — it **hollows you quietly**.

Until one day, you forget:
- What you believe
- What you want
- What you feel
- And who you ever were before the mask became your face

When Everything Is Sacred, Nothing Can Be True

We used to disagree.
Now we **worship**.

Not God. Not beauty. Not truth.
We worship **ourselves** — our feelings, our wounds, our identities, our narratives.
And we dare anyone to challenge us.

Because in this new moral order, **everything is sacred** —
except honesty.

Your pain is sacred.
Your pronouns are sacred.
Your trauma is sacred.
Your anger is sacred.
Your grief, your beliefs, your lived experience — all sacred.

Sacred doesn't mean respected anymore.
It means **untouchable**.

It means:

> "Don't question me."
> "Don't disagree with me."
> "Don't even ask — just affirm."

But here's the problem:

> When **everything is sacred**, nothing can be questioned.
> And when nothing can be questioned, **nothing can be true**.

We haven't built a more compassionate world.
We've built a shrine to **personal fragility**, guarded by shame, censorship, and applause.

We say we want dialogue, but we've outlawed challenge.
We say we want understanding, but we've criminalized complexity.
We say we want truth — but only if it kneels at the altar of emotion.

And so reality becomes a hostage of performance.
We trade sharp edges for soft language.
We call correction "violence."
We call disagreement "erasure."
We call silence "allyship."

We strip words of meaning until truth is no longer offensive — because it's no longer spoken.

But the soul knows.
The body knows.
Some part of you has always known:

> You were not built to live inside a shrine of unchallenged identity.
> You were built to live inside **truth** — raw, risky, offensive, sacred only because it's real.

And real truth doesn't flatter you.
It **transforms you**.

Not by affirming your every feeling,
but by confronting the lies you've told yourself to survive.

This Isn't a Book of Solutions — It's a Book of Exposure

You've probably noticed by now:
This book doesn't offer steps.
It doesn't offer strategies.

There's no 5-point plan to rebuild society.
No workbook to become your "authentic self."

That was never the point.

> This isn't a book of solutions.
> It's a book of **exposure**.

Its job was to show you the mirror —
not tell you what to do with the reflection.

Because most of what we call "solutions" today
are just **new performances** in more therapeutic language.
- You quit the job, but keep the mask.
- You leave the tribe, but find a new one to impress.
- You change your pronouns, your politics, your practices — but never ask: *Am I living from fear or from truth?*

So no, this book doesn't hand you a roadmap.
It hands you something far more disturbing:

> *Yourself.*
> Unperformed.
> Unfiltered.
> Unarmed.

What you do from here — that's on you.
Not the version of you you've crafted for applause.
Not the version that's been rewarded for emotional safety.

You.
The one who knows when you're faking.
The one who winces when you lie.
The one who still whispers, *"That's not true for me."*
Even when you pretend it is.

This book doesn't need to tell you what's next.
Because if you've been paying attention, you already know.

You don't need a plan.
You need to stop performing.
And start listening to the voice you've buried under a lifetime of applause.

Reclaiming the Self Isn't Revolution — It's Return

Reclaiming your self won't look radical.
It won't go viral.
It won't earn you a standing ovation.

There's no badge for it.
No tribe to welcome you back.
No script for how to do it correctly.

> Because reclaiming your self isn't a revolution.
> It's a **return** — to what was buried beneath the performance.

You will not be rewarded.
You may be misunderstood.
You may be called cold, distant, difficult, dangerous.
You may lose friends who never knew you — only the version of you they approved of.

But what you gain is something infinitely more rare:

> *The ability to hear yourself again.*

To feel something true and **not flinch.**
To speak and **not scan for reaction.**
To live without constantly managing the optics of your own existence.

This isn't about being edgy.
It's not about being rebellious or "based" or countercultural.

It's about becoming real.

It's about waking up one day and saying:

> *"I'm not performing this anymore."*
> *"I'm not curating this."*
> *"I'm done translating myself into something likable."*

You'll feel raw.
Exposed.
Uncertain.
But underneath that?

A pulse. A breath.
A voice — faint, but yours.
And maybe for the first time in years, **it won't be acting.**

That's not revolution.
It's *remembering*.

Don't Raise the Flag — Hold the Mirror

There is no flag worth raising if it requires you to lie.
No moral banner worth waving if it erases your voice to keep you included.
No ideology worth serving if it demands your personality be edited into compliance.

> You were not born to be branded.
> You were not meant to be a mascot for movements.
> You were not built to be a mouthpiece for emotional consensus.

You were meant to tell the truth.
To feel your own instincts.
To wrestle. To doubt. To stand. To fall. To own it.

And in a world screaming for symbolic allegiance,
the most radical thing you can do is simple:

> Don't raise the flag.
> **Hold the mirror.**

Not to others — to yourself.
Look at what you've said to fit in.
Look at what you've silenced to feel safe.
Look at who you've become to be loved.

And don't run from what you see.

Because when you stop performing,
when you finally choose discomfort over disguise,
when you choose truth over tribal applause —
something shatters.

And what's left isn't a brand.
It's not a costume.
It's not a moral image.

It's you. And you are enough to begin again.

Case Study: You

You used to say what you thought.
Before you learned what would get applause.

You used to feel things fully.
Before you learned which feelings were acceptable.

You used to ask hard questions.
Before you realized questions made people uncomfortable.

You used to tell the truth.
Before you saw what happened to the last person who did.

You still remember who you were.
You haven't lost it.
You've just been editing it.

To be liked.
To be safe.
To be seen as good.

But now you see the cost.
And now, maybe,
you're ready to stop performing the version of yourself that survives the room.

And start being the one who walks out of it —
with your integrity intact.

Closing Paragraph

If this book has done anything, let it be this:
Let it take the version of you that was built to survive —
the version made of curated opinions, secondhand language, borrowed beliefs, practiced empathy, and emotional safety —
and let it **burn**.

Not because that version was fake,
but because it was **too small** for who you were meant to become.

You were not built to be liked.
You were not built to be correct.
You were not built to be softly consumed by consensus.

You were built to **feel the full weight of being human** —
to carry contradiction,
to stand alone when it matters,
to speak when your voice shakes,
to love without strategy,
to walk away from applause when it costs you your soul.

You were built to remember — not invent — who you are.
To return, not reinvent.
To hold the mirror, even when what you see is fractured and hard and nothing like the image you've sold to the world.

The truth won't make you a hero.
It won't make you popular.
It won't make you safe.

But it will make you **whole**.

So no — this book won't tell you who to be.
It won't give you new lines to memorize or new masks to wear.

It will only ask you one question —
the same question you've been avoiding every time you stayed quiet,
smiled when you didn't mean it,
or nodded when you wanted to scream:

> *What would your life look like if you stopped performing?*

If that question makes your heart race,
you're not broken.
You're waking up.

And if there's any voice left in you —
the quiet, unruly, unbranded one —
listen.

Because that voice is not here to impress.
It's here to **liberate** you.

And the next chapter of your life?
It begins when you stop writing for the crowd
and start telling the truth —
even if your voice is the only one that echoes back.

◆ ◆ ◆

Acknowledgement

To my wife, Mel — your strength holds everything together. While I wandered through the fog of ideas and confrontation, you kept the home stable, safe, and standing. Your presence is power. This book would not exist without your quiet force behind me.

To my kids — Barnaby, Olli, Pickle, and Turtle — you are my compass. You're the reason I never stop trying to build something better, even when it feels impossible. I hope one day you read this and understand not just the world I saw, but why I refused to lie about it.

To my parents, Sue and Kevin — the most kind, supportive, and grounded souls I've ever known. Your steadiness is a light I've leaned on more than you realize.

To the mates who never forget to check in, who make space for me in their lives, and who remind me who I am when the noise gets loud — thank you. You help me stay real when everything else is performance. And to the reader — if you made it this far, it means something inside you refused to be polite. I wrote this for you.

About The Author

Glenn Davies

Glenn Davies is a lifelong observer of the human condition — someone drawn not just to what people say, but to the quiet patterns underneath what they do.

With a natural interest in psychology, social dynamics, and cultural behaviour, he's spent decades watching people across borders, ideologies, and systems — always asking: What makes us tick? What makes us follow, betray, perform, or stay silent?

Glenn brings the mind of an informal behavioural analyst and the curiosity of a Cultural observer into every word he writes. His background in leadership, global ventures, and navigating diverse cultures has exposed him to both the surface and subterranean forces that shape modern human behaviour — from boardrooms to belief systems.

He is especially interested in the space where morality collapses into performance, and where identity becomes costume. The Moral Illusion is the result of years spent interrogating not just others, but himself — peeling back the polished layers we all wear to survive approval, and asking what remains underneath when the audience stops clapping.

He lives between Japan and Singapore with his wife and children — and writes for those who are tired of pretending.

www.ingramcontent.com/pod-product-compliance
Lightning Source LLC
Chambersburg PA
CBHW052206090526
44583CB00017BA/2172